Light A Big Fire

The Complete Guide to Building eBooks

All you need to know about formatting and building Kindle eBooks.
Includes 6 step by step tutorials on formatting and building eBooks.

Peter Reynolds

CONTENTS

1	LIGHT A BIG FIRE	1
2	FORMATTING YOUR BOOK IN MICROSOFT WORD	2
3	CREATING AN EBOOK COVER	10
4	OPF, NCX, HTML, XHTML AND CSS	11
5	BUILDING A KINDLE FORMAT 8 EBOOK	19
6	TUTORIAL 1 - CREATING A KINDLE EBOOK	25
7	TUTORIAL 2 - CREATING A CHILDREN'S BOOK WITH KINDLE FORMAT 8	35
8	MORE FORMATTING TECHNIQUES	44
9	THE EPUB FORMAT	53
10	TUTORIAL 3 - CREATING AN EPUB EBOOK	55
11	TUTORIAL 4 CONVERTING THE EPUB 2 BOOK TO EPUB 3	65
12	CALIBRE	71
13	TUTORIAL 5 BUILDING AN EBOOK WITH CALIBRE	84
14	SIGIL	88
15	TUTORIAL 6 BUILDING AN EBOOK WITH SIGIL	92
16	PUBLISHING YOUR BOOK	97
	RESOURCES	99
	ABOUT THE AUTHOR	100

1 LIGHT A BIG FIRE

Writing and publishing your own book is exciting. Throughout history people have lit big fires to celebrate great achievements. I have chosen this name for this book because it is about helping people achieve something very spectacular - writing and publishing their own book. I also like the imagery Amazon have used in naming their eReader, Kindle.

This book is both a reference and a how to manual. I have tried to avoid padding the book and concentrate on information which can be used by you to build your books.

This book can be used at a number of different levels. In this book we will discuss the following topics:

- Formatting a eBook in Microsoft Word

- Converting to HTML

- Using Amazon to convert your eBook for the Kindle

- An advanced guide to Kindle Format 8

- Tutorials for Kindle Format 8

- An advanced guide to the EPUB format

- Tutorials for EPUB

- Using Calibre for creating eBooks

- Using Sigil to create eBooks

- Publishing your book on Amazon, Barnes and Noble and other stores

I am presume that most people who buy this book will use it both as a reference and to learn about creating eBooks. However, I would like to suggest some routes through the book depending on what you want to do:

I know little about HTML and just want to get my eBook published for the Kindle

Read the section on *formatting in Microsoft Word*, *Using Amazon to convert your book* and the section on *publishing on KDP* (Kindle Direct Publishing)

I know little about HTML and just want to get my eBook published in the EPUB format and for the Kindle

Read the section on formatting in *Microsoft Word*, *Sigil* and the section on *publishing your eBook*

I already know how to format my book but I would like to know how I can fully use Kindle Format 8

Read the section on the *OPF, NCX, HTML, XHTML and CSS* and *Kindle Format 8*

I want to learn more about the EPUB format

Read the section on the *OPF, NCX, HTML, XHTML and CSS* and the *EPUB format* and *EPUB tutorials*.

2 FORMATTING YOUR BOOK IN MICROSOFT WORD

Less is more

The first thing you should remember is that your book will be seen in a variety of different devices and even different people using the same device may use different fonts or font size. The best way to ensure that your eBook looks good on all devices is to be sparing with formatting. Different font sizes may work perfectly on a printed document but are not helpful in an eBook. You should ensure that the text in the book is formatted using the normal style with the exception of chapter headings and text you wish to highlight.

AaBbCcDd	AaBbCcDd	AaBbCc
¶ Normal	¶ No Spac...	Heading 1

You should also avoid complicated tables, columns and graphics which are bigger than the smallest eReader screen. You should think carefully before adding a formatting effect and only include it if it will add something significant to the book.

The techniques in this chapter were written for Word 2010 and Word 2013 but you will be able to use them for other version of Word or other word processors.

Setting up Word

It can very helpful to see formatting such as paragraph marks in your document. To do this go to the paragraph section of Home ribbon and select the paragraph mark.

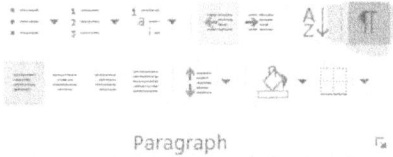

You will now see that all paragraph marks and line breaks within your document are highlighted.

Amazon recommends that you should indent the first line of each paragraph. To do this select the mark which is used to indicate further options in the Paragraph section of the Home ribbon.

This will open a dialog box where you can select that the first line be indented.

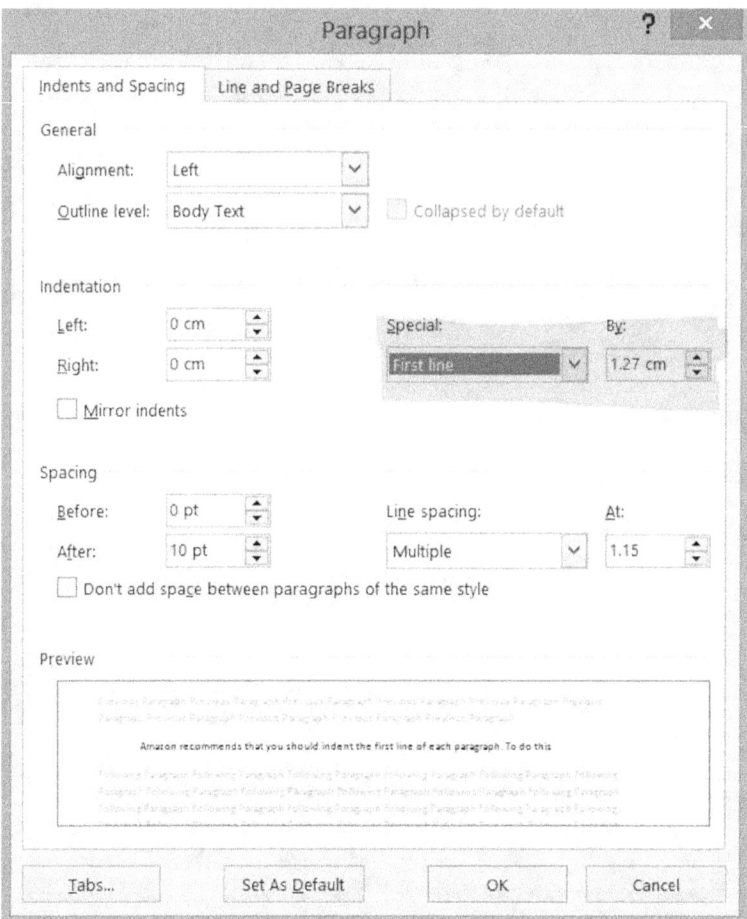

I have added an indent of 1.27 cm (0.5 inches).

Books and eBooks usually have the text justified on each side. To do this select a paragraph and select the justified text button from the Home ribbon. The subsequent paragraphs will be justified in the same way.

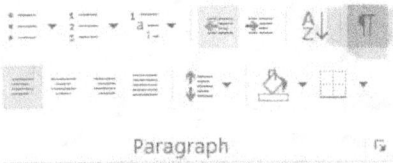

If you are already midway through your document and now want to change the formatting so that the first line is indented in all the paragraphs you can use the Format Painter button.

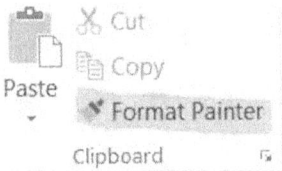

Highlight one paragraph making sure to include the end paragraph mark. Click on the Format Painter and then highlight the paragraphs you wish to change. If you click the Format Painter once it will make one change. If you double click on the Format Painter you will be able to continue making changes until you click on the Format Painter button once more to stop this.

One problem with Kindles is that if you insert a carriage return, you cannot be sure that it will appear correctly in all Kindle versions. Amazon recommend that you add a space after the carriage return. To do this select the icon for the paragraph dialog box and add a 10 pt spacing after the paragraph mark.

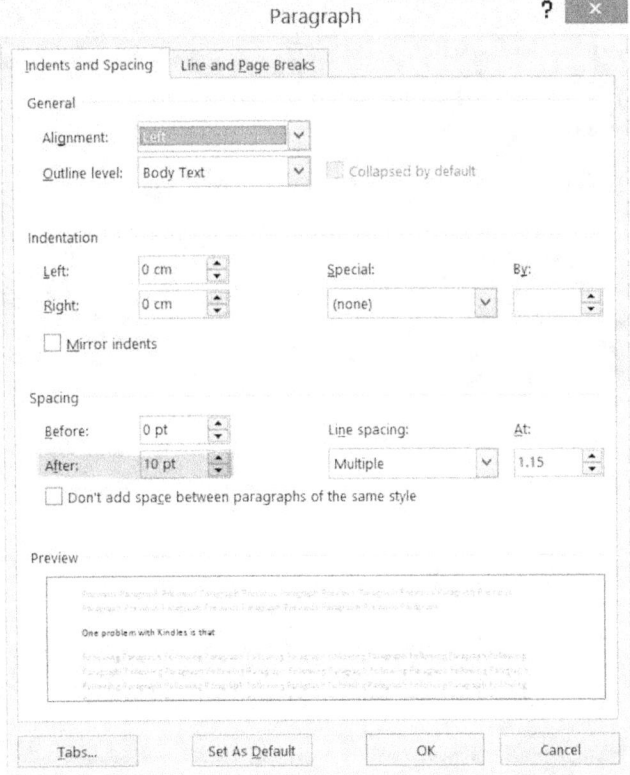

Chapter headings

Amazon recommends starting each chapter at the beginning of a new page. To this place you cursor just before the text you want to use as the chapter heading and select Ctrl + Enter. You can also do by inserting a page break from the Insert ribbon.

You should always use the heading 1 style for your chapter headings. To do this highlight the text you want as header and select the style Heading 1.

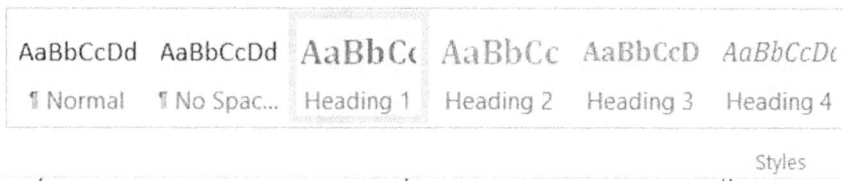

If you have sub headings within a chapter you should use Heading 2 and so.

Another advantage of using this is that when you create a Table of Contents within Word you can automatically use the chapter headings.

Spaces

When working in a document the writer sometimes inserts more than one space. In the Word or printed document this might not be noticeable but it can be a problem in an eBook. I would recommend getting rid of all cases with more than one space. To do this use Ctrl+H to open Find & Replace dialog. In the find box enter two spaces and in the replace box enter one space. You may have to click the replace all button more than once. If for example there are three spaces the first time you do a replace all, one of the three spaces will be removed leaving two spaces. You know that all your spaces are single spaces when you press the replace all button and its says there are no spaces to replace.

Copy/ Paste

One of the problems with Word is that if you copy from one document to another you copy the formatting information as well as the text. I would recommend you use the Paste As Text option. To do this select the position you want to insert the text and right click. In the menu you will see an entry Paste Options. If you choose the icon with a clipboard and the letter A in the bottom right hand corner you will insert the text as plain text and the formatting will come from your document rather than the document which the text was copied from.

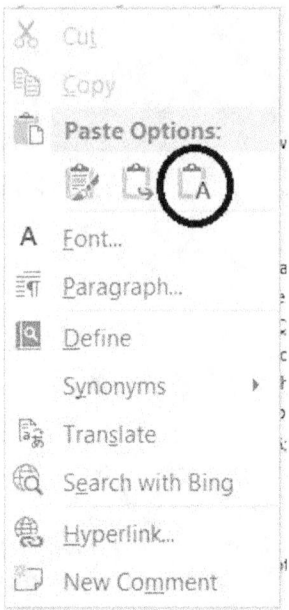

Pictures

When people are working in Word they often simply copy a picture. You should avoid doing this when you are formatting a book for a Kindle and instead go to the Insert ribbon and select Insert Picture.

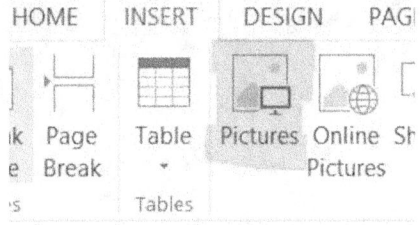

Insert Hyperlinks

If you type a URL into your document, Word will recognize what it is and covert it to a hyperlink. However, you may want to use a descriptive text rather than a URL or you may want to have a link to somewhere else in the book.

To insert a hyperlink with different text select the Hyperlink icon from the Insert ribbon.

The hyperlink dialog box will open.

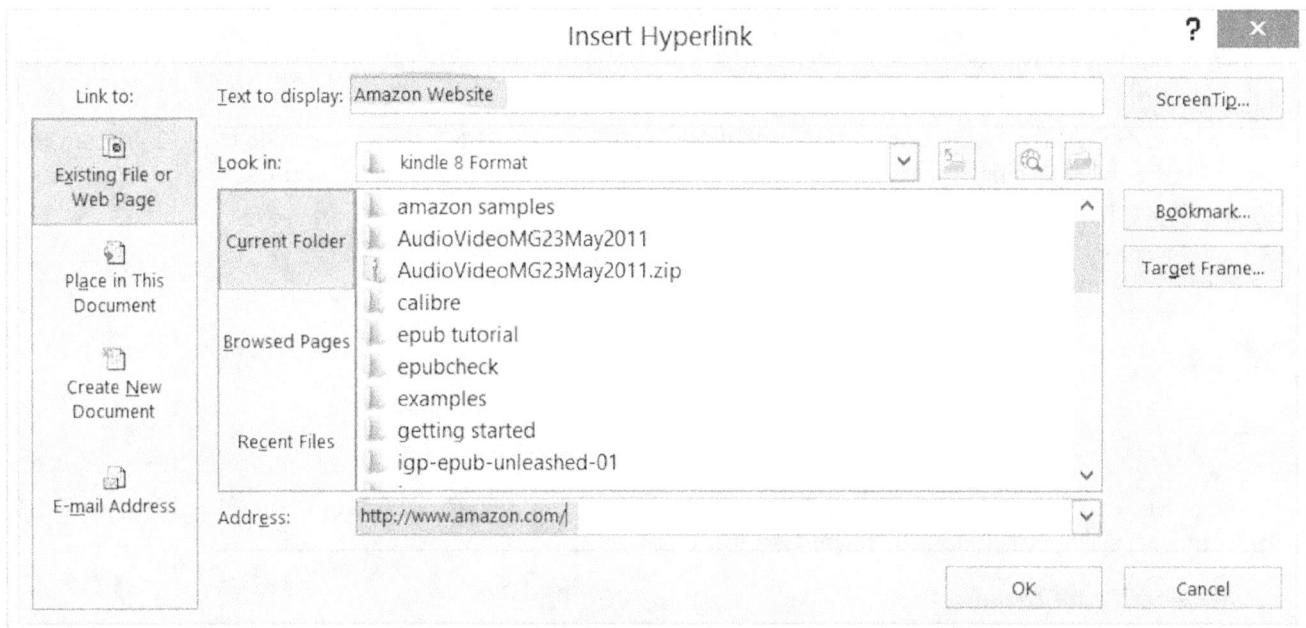

In the box "Text to display" you insert the text you wish to use and you insert the URL in the "Address"box.

To insert a link within the book select the Bookmarks button from the Insert Hyperlink dialog. You will see the chapter and other headings and you can select one of these as the place the link will be to. The text will be taken from your heading or you can enter new text.

If you wish to have a link to somewhere in your document which has not in the list of headings you can first insert a bookmark and then link to this.

Title, Copyright, Dedication, Preface and Table of Contents

Amazon use a separate image file as the cover of your book but they recommend having separate pages for the title, copyright, dedication, preface and Table of Contents. Some authors recommend putting some of these on the same page to save space. The reason for this is that when someone is looking at your book and deciding whether to buy it they will probably use the function on the Amazon site where you can have a preview of the book. This function only previews the first few pages so if you have a page for each of these that will take a lot of your preview space. However, this is up to you.

Amazon recommend having separate pages for title, copyright and dedication. In their books "Building Your Book for Kindle" and "Building Your Book for Kindle for Mac" they recommend centering and highlighting the text.

An example of the title page would be:

Light A Big Fire

The complete guide to building eBooks

By Peter Reynolds

An example of the copyright page would be:

Copyright © 2013 Peter Reynolds

An example of the dedication page would be:

To my family with thanks for putting up with me when I was writing this book.

If you have preface or prologue page it should come after this. My comment about thinking of having the title, copyright and dedication on the same page is not relevant to the preface as this usually contains material which will interest prospective readers.

To insert a Table of Contents you should firstly check that the items you want to include in the Table of Contents have got the style Heading 1 or Heading 2. You then position the cursor where you want the Table of Contents to be by selecting the Table of Contents icon from the Reference ribbon.

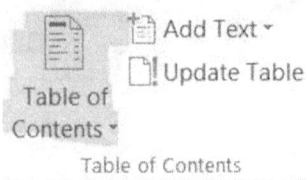

You will see a menu containing a number of choices which you can select. You can also select the "Custom Table of Contents" dialog by selecting the second last menu option.

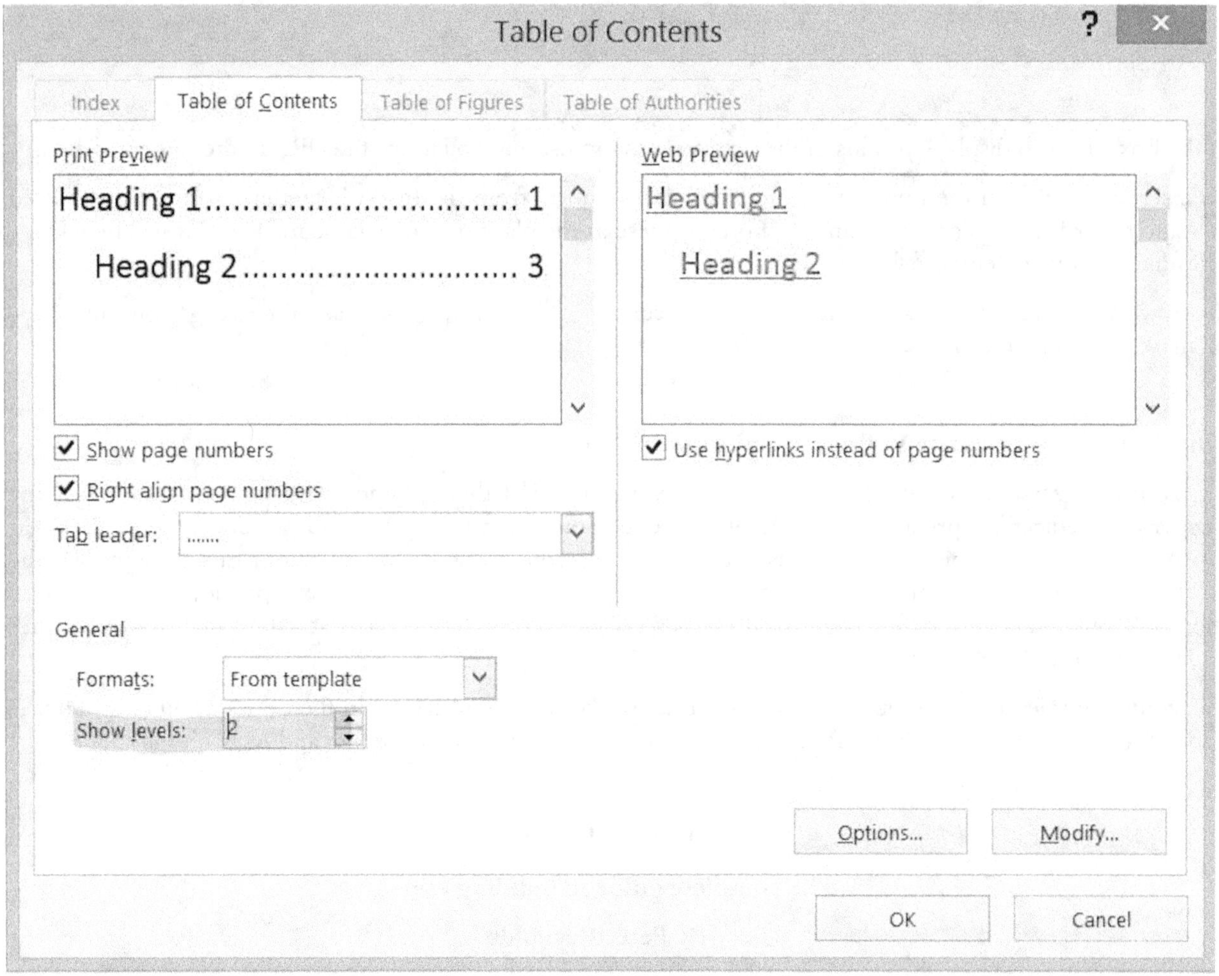

In this dialog box I have decided to only show first and second levels. It is possible to have more less levels as you wish. When the Table of Contents appears it is also possible to remove text from it.

If you later edit the document but do not change the headings you can right click on the Table of Contents and get Word to update the page numbers only.

USING AMAZON TO CONVERT WORD TO KF8

Amazon and Smash Words both offer the facility to upload a Microsft Word document and have this converted to their ebook format. Amazon also allow their Kindle customers to send a file to their Kindle email address and if they have "convert" in the subject line the document will be converted to the Kinle format.

You can find your Kindle email address on the Manage your Kindle pages. More information on Amazon's personal document service is available from here: http://www.amazon.com/gp/help/customer/display.html/ref=help_search_1-5?ie=UTF8&nodeId=201245220&qid=1375644567&sr=1-5. If there is a problem with this link just type "personal documents" in the search on Amazon Help. This conversion is useful to use if you intend submitting a Word document to Amazon.

3 CREATING AN EBOOK COVER

The saying that you cannot tell a book from its cover may be true but the cover is the first thing people see and it can sell your book. It is very important that you get this right. There is a very good argument for getting a professional design for your book. On websites such as http://www.guru.com/ you might be able to find a freelance graphic artist who is not so expensive. If you decide to do this put thought into the briefing that you will give the graphic artist. They are unlikely to read your book before they start trying to decide how to represent it.

Amazon have a cover creator tool on their website. When you uploading your book you can decide to use the cover creator. this is a three step wizard to creating your cover. You first choose the image then the design and enter your text. You then preview it and if you like what you see go ahead and if not you can start again.

The file for your cover should be either a.jpg or .tif file. The files must be at least 1000 pixels on its longest side and should have the height/ width ratio of 1.6. Amazon give an example of 1000 by 1600.

The cover needs to have the title of the book and the name of the author.

You should not include your cover as part of your book.

4 OPF, NCX, HTML, XHTML AND CSS

Kindle Format 8 uses the same set of files to create eBooks as the Mobi or EPUB formats. The difference is that Kindle Format 8 and EPUB 3 provide a much richer set of functionality. I am going to take the Kindle Format 8 perspective as I introduce these files and later will deal with them from the EPUB perspective. The files used in Kindle Format 8 are:

- OPF - The OPF (Open Package Format) defines how all the different elements in an eBook are put together.

- NCX - The NCX (Navigation Control for XML) enable you to use a table of contents and other navigation controls. This format has been deprecated in EPUB 3 which uses the HTML5 element

- HTML - This is where the content of the book is.

- CSS - CSS (Cascading Style Sheets) are where the formatting information is kept.

The Kindle Format 8 and Mobi use the same source files as for EPUB files. This makes it possible to use the same source for eBooks intended for the Kindle and for other eReaders.

Warning: Both OPF and NCX files are XML and are case-sensitive. This is particularly important when using elements in these files. For example the element in the NCX file has a capital 'M' in the middle.

OPF

The OPF (Open Package Format) defines how all the different elements in an eBook are put together. This is where you put information about where the content is, the metadata, how the eBook is ordered, and functionality which helps you go to certain sections within the eBook.

The main element in the OPF file is the element and this has four child elements metadata, manifest, spine, and guide.

metadata - This is where the metadata about the book such as the its title, author's name, publisher etc. are stored. The metadata items use Dublin Core terms to define the metadata. The Dublin (Ohio not Ireland) Core is metadata used to identify document and books. The Simple Dublin Core Metadata Element Set (DCMES) consists of 15 metadata elements:

- Title

- Creator

- Subject

- Description

- Publisher

- Contributor

- Date

- Type

- Format

- Identifier

- Source

- Language

- Relation

- Coverage

- Rights

All of these can be used as metadata in an eBook. The Dublin Core is the reason why the word 'creator' is used instead of 'author' in eBook medata.

manifest - is a list of all the files which are contained in the book. This includes content such as HTML files as well as the graphic file used for the cover.

The item element in the manifest section has three required attributes:

href - the address where the asset is

id - This must be unique identifier and should follow the same syntax conventions as id values in HTML (i.e. must start with a letter, must not have special characters, and it must be unique).

media-type - the MIME Type (or Internet Media Type) of the asset.

The following are a list of some of the media-type which could be used in an eBook:

- toc.ncx Meta TOC File - application/x-dtbncx+xml
- .html Content files - application/xhtml+xml
- .CSS Stylesheets - text/CSS
- .jpg, .jpeg, or .jpe images - image/jpeg
- .png images - image/png
- .gif images - image/gif
- .svg images - image/svg+xml
- .ttf True Type Fonts - font/truetype
- .otf OpenType Fonts - font/opentype
- .mp3 Audio file - audio/mpeg
- .mp4 Video File - video/mp4

spine - The spine lists all the HTML documents in the order they are read if you read from start to finish.

guide - The "Go To..." functionality in the Kindle allows readers to go to locations such as the cover, table of contents, beginning or end. The guide section contains element which identifies structural components of the eBook and allow readers to go to that place in the eBook. This element is optional.

OPF example

This is the OPF file which we will use later for first tutorial.

```
<?xml version="1.0" encoding="iso-8859-1"?>

  <package unique-identifier="uid" xmlns:opf="http://www.idpf.org/2007/opf"
xmlns:asd="http://www.idpf.org/asdfaf">
```

This is this is the XML declaration which gives the address where the schema for OPF can be found.

```
<metadata>

  <dc-metadata xmlns:dc="http://purl.org/metadata/dublin_core"
xmlns:oebpackage="http://openeBook.org/namespaces/oeb-package/1.0/">

  <dc:title>The Adventures of Sherlock Holmes</dc:title>

  <dc:language>en</dc:language>

  <dc:creator>Sir Arthur Conan Doyle</dc:creator>

  <meta name="cover" content="SH_cover" />

  <x-metadata>

  <EmbeddedCover>images/SherlockCover.jpg</EmbeddedCover>

  </x-metadata>

  </dc-metadata>
```

</metadata>

This is the metadata element where the book's metadata is stored.

NOTE: The use of name="cover" in the metadata element name is mandatory.

<p class="lft"><manifest>

<item id="content" media-type="text/x-oeb1-document" href="toc.html"></item>

<item id="ncx" media-type="application/x-dtbncx+xml" href="toc.ncx"></item>

<item id="Adventure1" media-type="text/x-oeb1-document" href="adventure1.html"></item>

<item id="Adventure2" media-type="text/x-oeb1-document" href="adventure2.html"></item>

<manifest>

 <item id="content" media-type="text/x-oeb1-document" href="toc.html"></item>

 <item id="ncx" media-type="application/x-dtbncx+xml" href="toc.ncx"></item>

 <item id="Adventure1" media-type="text/x-oeb1-document" href="adventure1.html"></item>

 <item id="Adventure2" media-type="text/x-oeb1-document" href="adventure2.html"></item>

<item id="Adventure12" media-type="text/x-oeb1-document" href="adventure12.html"></item>

 </manifest>

The manifest element is where the files which make up the book are listed. The id attribute in the <item> element above is used as the idref attribute in the <itemref> element below.

<spine toc="ncx">

 <itemref idref="Adventure1"/>

 <itemref idref="Adventure2"/>

<itemref idref="Adventure12"/> </spine>

The <spine> element lists the reading order for the book. The attribute toc in the <spine> element uses the reference ncx for the table of contents.

<guide>

<reference type="toc" title="Table of Contents" href="toc.html"/>

</guide>

In eReaders such as a Kindle there is the facility to go to certain sections of the book. In this example we enable the Table of Contents to be accessed in this way.

TABLE OF CONTENT & NCX

There are also two files which are used to provide the table of contents. One of these is a HTML file which represents what the table of contents will look like and the other is the NCX file. This stands for Navigation Control for XML. The NCX format was created by the Daisy Consortium and is used for navigation control in Kindle Format 8, MOBI and EPUB.

The HTML Table of Contents file is simply a list of links to the relevant content.

```
<h1 id="toc">Table of Contents</h1>
<ul>
<li><a href="adventure1.html">ADVENTURE I. A SCANDAL IN BOHEMIA</a></li>

<li><a href="adventure12.html">ADVENTURE XII. THE ADVENTURE OF THE COPPER BEECHES</a></li>
</ul>
```

This example shows the header in a <h1> element and the chapter between <a href> elements. Each of the chapter names use a <a href> element which links to the start of that chapter.

The NCX file is an XML file which contains the navigation controls. When creating an EPUB book there are some metadata entries such as the unique identifier, usually the ISBN, which are mandatory. This metadata section is not used in the Kindle formats.

```
<?xml version="1.0"?>
<!DOCTYPE ncx PUBLIC "-//NISO//DTD ncx 2005-1//EN"
"http://www.daisy.org/z3986/2005/ncx-2005-1.dtd">
<ncx xmlns="http://www.daisy.org/z3986/2005/ncx/" version="2005-1">
```

The header section of the NCX file and the <ncx> element specify the relevant namespace which is created and maintained by the DAISY Organization.

```
<docTitle>
<text>The Adventures of Sherlock Holmes</text>
</docTitle>
<docAuthor>
<text>Sir Arthur Conan Doyle</text>
</docAuthor>
```

One of the differences between EPUB and the formats used by Amazon, MOBI and Kindle Format 8 is that the EPUB format requires that some of the metadata used in the OPF file is repeated here. The Amazon formats do not require this and you can see the example above we have included the metadata for the Title (docTitle) and for the Author (docAuthor).

```
<navMap>
<navPoint id="navpoint-1" playOrder="1">
<navLabel>
<text>ADVENTURE I. A SCANDAL IN BOHEMIA</text>
</navLabel>
<content src="adventure1.html"/>
</navPoint>


</navMap>
```

The Navigation Map <navMap> is comprised of one or more <navPoint> elements. Each <navPoint> element declares three things:

The text for the hyperlink as it will appear in the Kindle. This is contained within the <navLabel> elements. The actual text appears contained in the element <text>.

Where the asset is. This is done using the <content> element which is a child element of <navPoint>. The src attribute contain the address of the asset in relation to the NCX file.

The play order. The playOrder attribute is an attribute of the <navPoint> and this provides the information the reader needs for next or previous buttons. Each <navPoint> element must a unique number for the playOrder value. <navPoint> also has an identifier which must be unique.

In previous MOBI formats a cover was added as a graphic file while in EPUB formats you could add it as HTML with the graphic as well as the Graphic itself. With Kindle Format 8 it is possible to add a HTML cover page. If you are doing this it might be a good idea to have it as the first item (playOrder="1").

HTML, XHTML AND CSS

HTML was an application of Standard Generalized Markup Language (SGML) which is a very flexible markup language framework. XHTML rewrote HTML 4 so that it was an application of XML which is a more restrictive markup language framework. XHTML documents, like all XML documents, must be well formed. This should:

- Have a single "root" element that contains all the other elements.

- Use only properly encoded legal Unicode characters.

- The begin, end, and empty-element tags that delimit the elements are correctly nested, with none missing and none overlapping.

- The element tags are case-sensitive; the beginning and end tags must match exactly. Tag names cannot contain any of the characters !"#$%&'()*+,/;?@[\]^`{|}~, nor a space character, and cannot start with -, ., or a numeric digit.

- None of the special syntax characters such as "<" and "&" appear except when performing their markup-delineation roles. XHTML documents use HTML entities to represent these characters. For example, < is used in the XHTML code and the browser shows "<".

HTML5 is an XML application and is intended to subsume not only HTML 4, but XHTML 1 and DOM Level 2 HTML as well.

CSS (Cascading Style Sheet) is a style sheet language used to describe the look and formatting of a document written in a markup language such as HTML5.

In the "How to" section of this book I will show how you can create some great effects for your Kindle Fire books.

One issue which you should bear in mind when working with CSS is that your book may be viewed on both Kindle Fire readers and on the early generation Kindle readers. These do not support the same range of CSS tags. In order to get round this it is possible to have use the '@media' tag to specify that one instance of a tag is for Kindle Format 8 while another instance of a tag with the same name is for MOBI 7. The tag @media followed by 'amzn-kf8' means that the code in the curly brackets immediately below are for Kindle Format 8 while 'amzn-mobi' means that it is intended for MOBI 7.

```
@media amzn-kf8

 {

.mediaExampleBorder

 {

border-radius: 1em;

padding: 1% 2%;

background: #CED3D0;

 }

 }


 @media amzn-mobi

 {

P.mediaExampleBorder

 {

font-size:3em;

font-weight: bold;

 }

 }
```

The example in the box shows code for creating a border with a background colour when using Kindle Format 8 and to make the text bigger and bold in MOBI 7. The following HTML can allow you to see this in practice using the Kindle Previewer.

```
<!DOCTYPE html>
<html xmlns="http://www.w3.org/1999/xhtml">
<head>
<title>test</title>
<link rel="stylesheet" href="style.CSS" type="text/CSS"/>
</head>
<body>
<p>some text before </p>
<p class="mediaExampleBorder">Some text in the middle </p>
<p>Some text after</p>
</body>
</html>
```

5 BUILDING A KINDLE FORMAT 8 EBOOK

With the launch of Kindle Fire, Amazon needed a more powerful eBook format in order to take advantage of the color screen and improved functionality. They went in a similar direction to IDPF who were working on EPUB 3 and decided to use HTML5 as the cornerstones of the new format. Kindle Format 8 is like EPUB in a number of ways:

- Both formats recognize a sizeable subset of HTML5 and CSS3

- Both formats uses OPF as the package file

- Both Kindle Format 8 and EPUB 2 uses NCX for the navigation information.

They differ in how they deal with some information which is required in the OPF or NCX file by one format by one format and not by the other, the Kindle format likes but does not insist on XHTML while EPUB does and in how the actual file is built.

The EPUB format is built by placing the component files in particular folders and compressing these folders into a single file with the extension .EPUB.

Kindle Format 8 is a compiled rather than compressed and in the compiled .mobi file which Kindlegen produces you have a Kindle Format 8 file and a MOBI 7 file for backward compatibility. When you publish your eBook you publish this MOBI file. A customers buying with a Kindle Fire get an AZW file which is Kindle Format 8. A customer with an older Kindle gets an AZW file which is MOBI 7. AZW format can be DRM (Digital Rights Management) restricted and locked to the device id which is registered automatically with the user account of the Kindle purchaser. DRM free books also carry the AZW extension but they are no different from MOBI files.

GETTING STARTED

There are a number of resources available on the Amazon and other websites which will help you creating books in Kindle Format 8. Amazon resource page for Kindle tools and samples is available here: www.amazon.com/kindleformat

Kindlegen is the tool which is used to generate the eBook. It is a command line tool and will be explained in more detail later in this book. The tool is available here: www.amazon.com/kindleformat/kindlegen

Kindle Previewer - This tools allows you to see how your book will appear in all versions of Kindle. The Kindle Previewer can also be used to create the eBook from an EPUB or HTML file. It is available from the Kindle Format page: www.amazon.com/kindleformat.

Kindle samples - Amazon provide a number of samples on the Kindle Format page, www.amazon.com/kindleformat , and it is well worth downloading and experimenting with these.

You should also obtain the Amazon Kindle Publishing Guide http://kindlegen.s3.amazonaws.com/AmazonKindlEPUBlishingGuidelines.pdf

A good HTML Editor is very and there are many tools to chose from. It is important that tool fully supports XHTML and HTML and can edit HTML, XML and CSS files. I would avoid a tool which did not allow you to edit the code as you would be better off with your Word Processor.

BUILDING YOUR KINDLE FORMAT 8 EBOOK

Kindlegen allows you to build a Kindle Format 8 from either a single HTML file or an OPF file. You can run Kindlegen by the command line or simple 'dropping' a file on it. If you try and open an OPF or HTML file in Kindle Previewer it will run Kindlegen first. When it is finished you can select to see the warning and other messages.

Command Line

Kindlegen is a command line program. This means that you run it by typing the command into the Command Prompt window. There are a number of potential problems with this. You may have your Kindlegen tool in one folder and your eBook files in another and the command line get very unwieldy. The best way to deal with this is to include the folder where you Kindlegen tool is within your computer's path directory. This will allow you to type 'Kindlegen' from any directory and the program will run.

Adding Kindlegen to your path folder in Microsoft Windows

In Windows 8 open the control panel, then select System. The dialog below will appear. In Windows 7 click on start button. You will see a link called 'Computer' on the right hand side. Right click on this and select Properties from the edit menu. The dialog box below will appear.

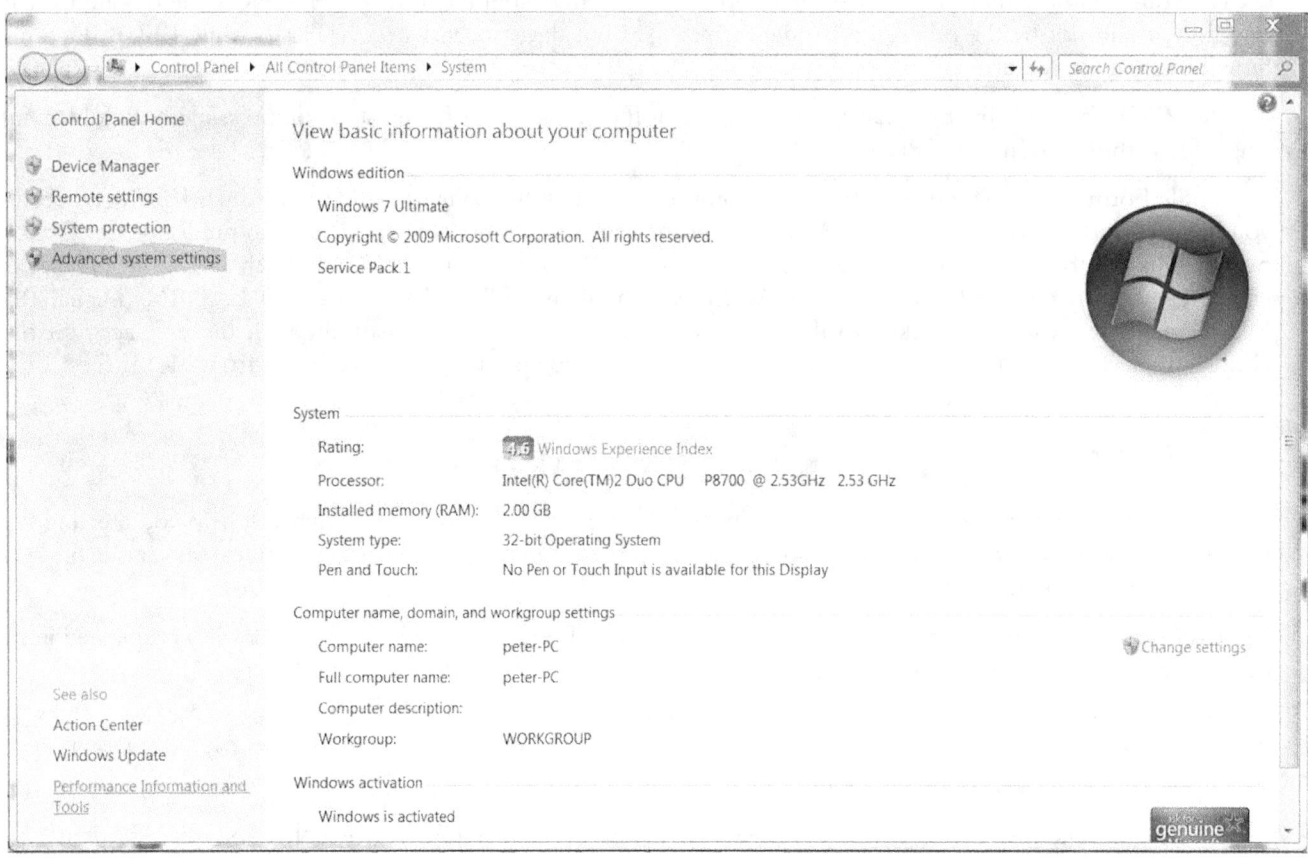

Click on Advanced System Settings.

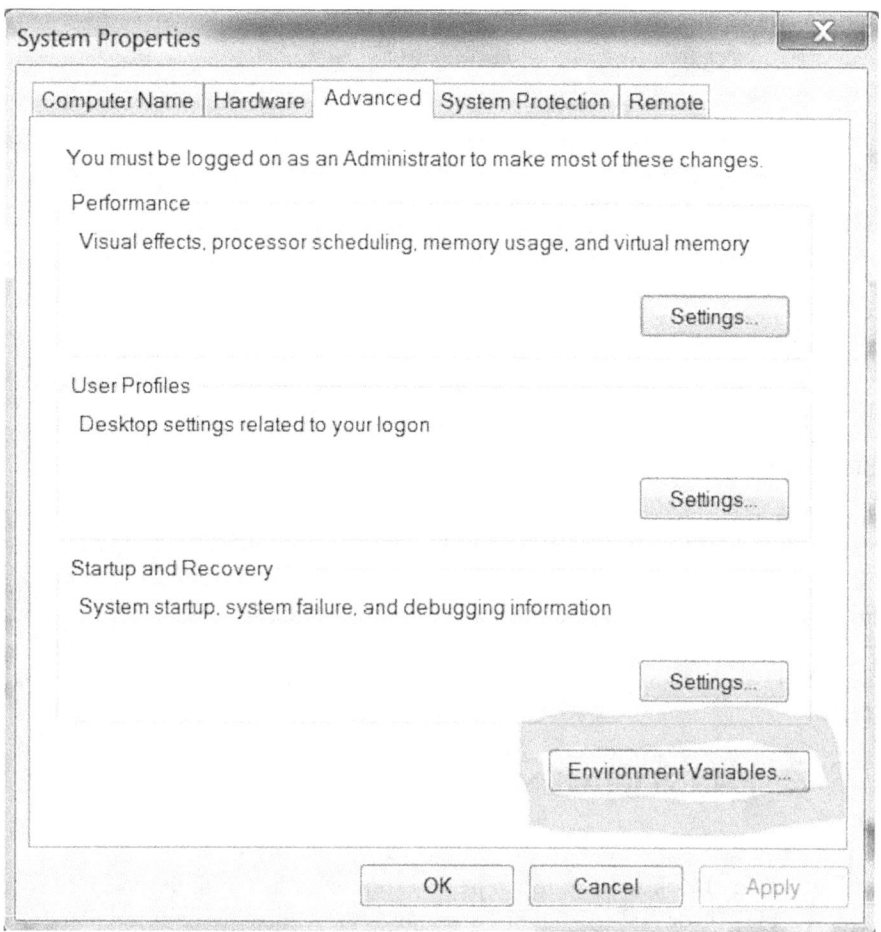

This will open the Advanced Tab of the System Properties dialog box. Click on the 'Environment Variables' button.

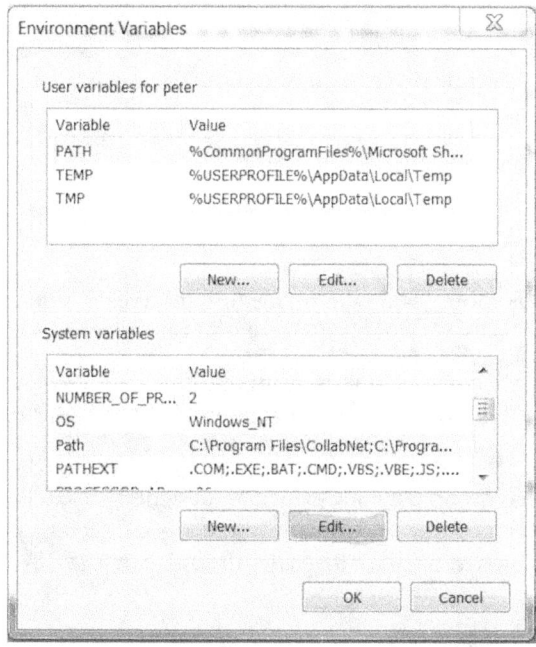

In the Environment Variables dialog select Path from the System variables window and select Edit.

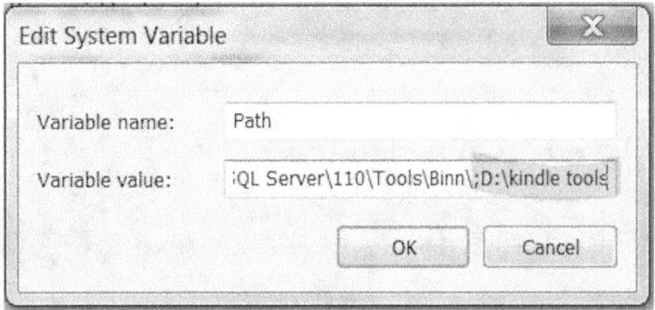

You should then add the folder where you keep your Kindlegen tool. If there are other values in the Variable value box you should insert a semi-colon before adding the folder name. I keep my Kindlegen tool in a folder in a folder 'D:\kindle tools'. You can see from the screen above that I have added the text ';D:\kindle tools'.

You should now confirm this change. Your system will have to be rebooted before this change takes place.

Opening Command Prompt Window

Windows provides a very simple way to open a Command Prompt Window at whatever folder you want. In Windows Explorer select the folder. Hold down the Shift Key and at the same time Right Click. You will see an option Open Command Prompt Here. Select this option and Command Prompt Window will be open at that Folder.

KINDLEGEN

Kindlegen options

To run the Kindlegen program and create an eBook your simply type the command line 'Kindlegen myfile.opf' It is possible for Kindlegen to convert a single HTML or XHTM file but using an OPF files allows you to create a book which is made up of a number of different HTML or XHTML files.

Kindlegen has a number of different compression options. You can instruct Kindlegen to use the compression by using either -c0, -c1 or -c2. These stand for:

- -c0: no compression

- -c1: standard DOC compression

- -c2: Kindle huffdic compression

You may want Kindlegen to create a file name which is different to the name of your source file. To do this you use -o followed by the file name you wish to use.

For example, the command line 'Kindlegen myfile.opf -o mybook.mobi ' will take myfile.opf and create an eBook called mybook.mobi.

The -verbose option lets you see everything that is happening when the eBook is being built. As Kindlegen has some very good error messages there is little to be gained from this you will see what is wrong from the error messages.

By default Kindlegen will generate UTF-8 content. This is a flavor of Unicode which is designed to have one character set for all human languages and for all computer platforms. Prior to Unicode there were different code pages depending on the character set used. The 1252 code page was one used for English and you can instruct Kindlegen to use by using the '-western' option.

The '-releasenotes' display the release notes for that version of Kindlegen.

The '-gif' option convert all images to the GIF format. The GIF format is smaller than some of the other image formats.

It is also possible to change the language you are operating Kindlegen in by using the option' -locale' followed by the two letter ISO 639 language code for the language you want to use. You can choose from English (en), German (de), French (fr), Italian (it) and Spanish (es). This option does not actually change the content of your eBook. What it does is allows you to see the error and warning messages which Kindlegen produces in another language.

Kindegen Errors and Warning

I have not been able to find a complete list of the errors and warning messages which Kindlegen will show. However, they are generally well written messages and worth investigating even if they are just warnings and an eBook has been created.

Errors are a problem which has prevented Kindlegen from creating the eBook, Warning are usually less serious problems which have occurred but have not prevented the eBook being created.

Examples of errors which will prevent a book being created include:

- Files referenced in the manifest section of the OPF not being found by Kindlegen.

- An eBook with the same name as the one you creating being already opened in Kindle Previewer or some similar application.

- Two items in the manifest having the same id.

- An ncx being referenced in the manifest but not being found.

Kindlegen gives good error messages. To solve the problem you simply read them and correct the problem.

Examples of warning messages which you might see include:

- There is a file referenced in the CSS or similar that cannot be found. (You may have copied a CSS file from another eBook and this used a background graphic which you were not planning to use with this eBook.

- A HTML element in one of the HTML files may not have been closed properly. (see below on resolving this error)

- The cover may be too small.

Kindlegen expects all HTML elements to having an opening and closing tag. If they have no closing tag, Kindlegen will insert one where it thinks it should be and give an error message such as:

'Warning(inputpreprocessor):W29004: Forcefully closed opened Tag: <p> in file: C:\myKindleProjects\page01.html   line: 0000038'

To resolve this error you open the file which has been highlighted as having the problem. The line number you see in the error message will be where Kindlegen expects the closing Tag to be. Go to this line and then look for the opening Tag in the lines before it. You should be able to see the Tag mentioned and put a closing Tag in the appropriate place.

It is important to go through these warning messages and get your source content as near to perfect as you can. Although Kindlegen has forced a correction which allows for the eBook to be created it may not look as good as it would do if you corrected the error.

KINDLEGEN FOR THE MAC

If you are using Kindlegen on a Mac you should do the following:

- Download the latest Kindlegen for the Mac from www.amazon.com/kindleformat/kindlegen This will usually be downloaded to your Downloads directory.

- Unzip the file. The browser may already have done this.

In order to use Kindlegen do the following:

Find the Kindlegen program and drag it to the Terminal window. The path name for Kindlegen will be entered automatically.

- If you run Kindlegen with no parameters you will see the instructions for the tool.

- To convert a book you can find the HTML or OPF file you want converted and drag it to the Terminal window where you previously dragged Kindlegen or you can type the command line Kindlegen followed by the path and name of the file. For example: kindlegen ~/Desktop/book.html

6 TUTORIAL 1 - CREATING A KINDLE EBOOK

We will use Sir Arthur Conan Doyle's collection of short stories, The Adventures of Sherlock Holmes, for our tutorial. I have included the text for this book, which is out of copyright, with the tutorial files available at http://www.epubservicesco.com/book.html

The Tutorial will show you how to do the following:

- Convert a book from text to HTML in your word processor

- Formatting the Chapters

- Structure the book

- Add a cover

- Add metadata

- Add illustrations

- Create a Kindle Format 8 eBook

CONVERT A BOOK FROM TEXT TO HTML IN YOUR WORD PROCESSOR

We will use Microsoft Word to add some basic HTML code and create a separate HTML file for each chapter.

Microsoft Word allows you to do a global search and replace. It is also possible to search or replace paragraph marks by using the characters: ^p.

The first thing I will do is replace any cases where there is more than one paragraph mark with a single paragraph mark. Using Ctrl+H I call the search and replace dialog box and put '^p^p' in the search field and '^p' in the replace field. This will find all instances where there are two paragraphs and replace them with a single paragraph mark. There may be cases where there were more than paragraph marks in a row and because of this I will keep running this search and replace until there are no cases of double paragraph marks found.

I will then use the search and replace dialog box again and put '^p' in the search field and '</p>^p<p>' in the replace field. This will insert a closing paragraph element at the end of each paragraph and an opening one at the beginning. I select replace all. When this is complete a dialog will ask me whether I want to do the search and replace for the whole document. I select no. I will also add one further <p> at the beginning of the document.

Create twelve HTML files which are labeled Adventure1.html, Adventure2.html and so on and add the following text to each of them.

```
<!DOCTYPE html>
<html xmlns="http://www.w3.org/1999/xhtml">
<head>
<title>Title</title>
<link type="text/CSS" href="styles.CSS" rel="Stylesheet"/></head>

<body>

</body>
</html>
```

Copy each Adventure from Microsoft Word to the appropriate HTML file. This can be done searching for the word 'Adventure' in Microsoft Word and going to the start of the next adventure, then bringing the cursor to the line before this and cut the text from there to the beginning of the document. You paste this text into the HTML file.

FORMATTING THE CHAPTERS

We want the chapters formatted with the title of the adventure in large text with a silhouette of Sherlock Holmes below it. Most of the text will formatted by simply inserting it between a start and end paragraph mark. The first word in each chapter will use drop capitals. I will also use the CSS file to have each paragraph indented and justified.

Open adventure1.html in my HTML editor. In the header of this and the other chapters there is an element title. This is the HTML element which gives a browser the title of the page you are viewing. Some Kindle devices also display this text. I will use the name of the book rather than the chapter name here and I copy "The Adventures of Sherlock Holmes" between the start and end <title> elements.

I shall put the title of the story with <h1> elements. This is equivalent to Heading 1 in Microsoft Word. I will use <h1> for the names of the stories and <h2> if there are chapters within one of the stories. One advantage of using CSS is that if at any stage I want to change how the chapter titles are displayed I just have to make one change to how the <h1> element is specified in the CSS file and it will format all titles the same way.

I will also add a graphic with a silhouette of Holmes after each title and split the title so that the number of the story is in the first line and the actual title starts on the second.

The code for this is as follows:

```
<h1>ADVENTURE I. - A SCANDAL IN BOHEMIA</h1>
<p> </p>
<p><img src="Holmes_with_glass.png" alt="Sherlock Holmes" /></p>
<h2>I.</h2>
```

The <h1> element which is used for the title is split by the line break element <br/>. The image is inserted using the HTML editor wizard for adding an image. This looks after the size etc. However, with the Kindle you could just leave out everything other than <img src="Holmes_with_glass.png" alt="" >.

The <h2> element is used to highlight the subsections in some of these stories.

I want to have the first word in each adventure as drop capitals. This feature is available for devices which use Kindle Format 8 such as Kindle Fire but it is not available for devices which use the older Mobi format such as the classic Kindle. We get around this by having two sets of code called span.dropcapA in our CSS file but differentitate them through the media query.

In the CSS file we will use the tag 'media="amzn-kf8"' to direct Kindlegen to use this for Kindle Format 8 and 'media="amzn-mobi"' for MOBI 7. This allows us to use drop capitals with Kindle Fire and Kindle Touch. Drop capitals cannot be used with classic Kindle so we simply make the word pronounced.

The code in the CSS for Kindle Format 8 is:

```
@media="amzn-kf8"
{
span.dropcapsA
{
float: left;
font-size: 4em;
font-weight: bold;
color:#000000;
margin-top: -.2em;
margin-bottom: -.2em;
margin-right: .1em;
padding-right: .1em;
text-shadow:5px -3px #151B54;
}
}
```

The code in the CSS for Mobi is:

```
@media="amzn-mobi"
{
span.dropcapsA
{
font-size: xx-large;
font-weight: bold;
color: #C11B17;
}
}
```

In the HTML file for each chapter we simply put the first word between <span> elements which deal with the drop capitals:

```
<p><span class="dropcapsA">"Holmes,"</span>
```

I have also added code in the CSS file which makes each paragraph indented by 50 px and justifies and modified the <h1> and <h2> elements. The <h1> and <h2> elements are centred and uppercase. I have added the code page-break-before:always; to the <h1> element. This will insert a page break immediately before this.

```
p {
text-indent:50px;
text-align: justify;
}

h1 {
font-size: 1.5em;
line-height: 1.33em;
text-align: center;
padding-bottom: 0em;
text-align: center;
text-transform: uppercase;
font-weight: normal;
letter-spacing: 4px;
page-break-before:always;
}
```

```
h2 {

    text-align: center;

    font-size: 1.33em;

    line-height: 1.2em;

    text-align: center;

    padding-bottom: 0em;

    text-align: center;

    text-transform: uppercase;

    font-weight: normal;

    letter-spacing: 3px;

}
```

STRUCTURE THE BOOK

We will use an OPF to provide the structure of the book and an NCX and HTML file to provide the navigation and table of contents for the book. We will start our work on the OPF file.

ADD A COVER

We have created a cover which is based on a graphic we have obtained from the The Sherlock Holmes Museum, 221b Baker Street, London, England, www.sherlock-holmes.co.uk. The text 'The Adventures of Sherlock Holmes' has been added at the top of this graphic and the name 'Sir Arthur Conan Doyle' has been added at the bottom. The graphic was saved as cover.png and the following line was added to the metadata section of the OPF file: <meta name="cover" content="SH_cover" /> and this line to the manifest of the OPF file: <item id="SH_cover" href="cover.png" media-type="image/png"></item>

ADD METADATA

In the metadata section we will add the title of the book, the author and the language. All of these use Dublin Core metadata terms.

We add the title by inserting the text between <dc:title> opening and closing tags.

<dc:title>The Adventures of Sherlock Holmes</dc:title>

In order to specify the language we use the ISO 639 language codes. Each language is given a code which will be universally understood by a machine processing the text. In this case the language is English so we use the code 'en'. Language codes are always written in lower case.

```
<dc:language>en</dc:language>
```

The author's name is inserted as creator of the work.

```
<dc:creator>Sir Arthur Conan Doyle</dc:creator>
```

If we had an ISBN number we would add it between <dc:identifier> tags. Amazon Kindle Direct Publishing does not require an ISBN and will allocate their identifier to the eBook when you publish it. Because of that we are not going to use this tag.

Table of Contents

When using a Table of Contents in a Kindle book you need two Table of contents files. toc.HTML is a HTML file and toc.ncx is an XML navigation file.

To create the toc.HTML we have the name of the book in a H1 element and an ordered list with links to each chapter in the order they appear and each link has the name of the chapter. This is shown below:

```
<ul>
 <li><a href="Adventure1.html">ADVENTURE I. A SCANDAL IN BOHEMIA</a></li>
 <li><a href="Adventure2.html">ADVENTURE II. THE RED-HEADED LEAGUE</a></li>
 <li><a href="Adventure3.html">ADVENTURE III. A CASE OF IDENTITY</a></li>
 <li><a href="Adventure4.html">ADVENTURE IV. THE BOSCOMBE VALLEY MYSTERY</a></li>
 <li><a href="Adventure5.html">ADVENTURE V. THE FIVE ORANGE PIPS</a></li>
 <li><a href="Adventure6.html">ADVENTURE VI. THE MAN WITH THE TWISTED LIP</a></li>
 <li><a href="Adventure7.html">ADVENTURE VII. THE ADVENTURE OF THE BLUE CARBUNCLE</a></li>
 <li><a href="Adventure8.html">ADVENTURE VIII. THE ADVENTURE OF THE SPECKLED BAND</a></li>
 <li><a href="Adventure9.html">ADVENTURE IX. THE ADVENTURE OF THE ENGINEER'S THUMB</a></li>
 <li><a href="Adventure10.html">ADVENTURE X. THE ADVENTURE OF THE NOBLE BACHELOR</a></li>
 <li><a href="Adventure11.html">ADVENTURE XI. THE ADVENTURE OF THE BERYL CORONET</a></li>
 <li><a href="Adventure12.html">ADVENTURE XII. THE ADVENTURE OF THE COPPER BEECHES</a></li>
 </ul>
```

To create the toc.ncx we add a navMap which comprises of a series of naPoints. This functionality lets us decide the order they appear and the navLabel gives us the text which is used. See below:

```
<navMap>

    <navPoint id="navpoint-1" playOrder="1"><navLabel><text>ADVENTURE I. A SCANDAL IN
BOHEMIA</text></navLabel><content src="Adventure1.html"/></navPoint>

    <navPoint id="navpoint-2" playOrder="2"><navLabel><text>ADVENTURE II. THE RED-HEADED
LEAGUE</text></navLabel><content src="Adventure2.html"/></navPoint>

    <navPoint id="navpoint-3" playOrder="3"><navLabel><text>ADVENTURE III. A CASE OF
IDENTITY</text></navLabel><content src="Adventure3.html"/></navPoint>

    <navPoint id="navpoint-4" playOrder="4"><navLabel><text>ADVENTURE IV. THE BOSCOMBE
VALLEY MYSTERY</text></navLabel><content src="Adventure4.html"/></navPoint>

    <navPoint id="navpoint-5" playOrder="5"><navLabel><text>ADVENTURE V. THE FIVE ORANGE
PIPS</text></navLabel><content src="Adventure5.html"/></navPoint>

    <navPoint id="navpoint-6" playOrder="6"><navLabel><text>ADVENTURE VI. THE MAN WITH THE
TWISTED LIP</text></navLabel><content src="Adventure6.html"/></navPoint>

    <navPoint id="navpoint-7" playOrder="7"><navLabel><text>ADVENTURE VII. THE ADVENTURE OF
THE BLUE CARBUNCLE</text></navLabel><content src="Adventure7.html"/></navPoint>

    <navPoint id="navpoint-8" playOrder="8"><navLabel><text>ADVENTURE VIII. THE ADVENTURE OF
THE SPECKLED BAND</text></navLabel><content src="Adventure8.html"/></navPoint>

    <navPoint id="navpoint-9" playOrder="9"><navLabel><text>ADVENTURE IX. THE ADVENTURE OF
THE ENGINEER'S THUMB</text></navLabel><content src="Adventure9.html"/></navPoint>

    <navPoint id="navpoint-10" playOrder="10"><navLabel><text>ADVENTURE X. THE ADVENTURE OF
THE NOBLE BACHELOR</text></navLabel><content src="Adventure10.html"/></navPoint>

    <navPoint id="navpoint-11" playOrder="11"><navLabel><text>ADVENTURE XI. THE ADVENTURE OF
THE BERYL CORONET</text></navLabel><content src="Adventure11.html"/></navPoint>

    <navPoint id="navpoint-12" playOrder="12"><navLabel><text>ADVENTURE XII. THE ADVENTURE
OF THE COPPER BEECHES</text></navLabel><content src="Adventure12.html"/></navPoint>

    </navMap>
```

Completing the OPF file and building the book

At this stage we should have 12 HTML files, a toc.HTML, a toc.ncx and a stylesheet, style.CSS.

We only have one style used in the stylesheet which is for Dropcaps. The stylesheet may simply have only the following contents:

```
@media amzn-mobi

{span.dropcapsA

{

font-size: xx-large;

font-weight: bold;

color: #C11B17;
```

```
}}

@media amzn-kf8
{ span.dropcapsA
{
float: left;
font-size: 4em;
font-weight: bold;
color:#000000;
margin-top: -.2em;
margin-bottom: -.2em;
margin-right: .1em;
padding-right: .1em;
text-shadow:5px -3px #151B54;
}}

p {
text-indent:50px;
text-align: justify;
}

h1 {
font-size: 1.5em;
line-height: 1.33em;
text-align: center;
padding-bottom: 0em;
text-align: center;
text-transform: uppercase;
font-weight: normal;
letter-spacing: 4px;
page-break-before:always;
}

h2 {
text-align: center;
font-size: 1.33em;
line-height: 1.2em;
```

```
text-align: center;

padding-bottom: 0em;

text-align: center;

text-transform: uppercase;

font-weight: normal;

letter-spacing: 3px;

}
```

This uses the @media direction to use a certain style depending on whether this is a KF8 or Mobi book.

We now need to complete the OPF file. The metadata section has already been completed so we need not to do any more here. In the manifest section we want to add all the files were using. The code below shows how this is done:

```
<manifest>
 <item id="content" media-type="text/x-oeb1-document" href="toc.html"></item>
 <item id="ncx" media-type="application/x-dtbncx+xml" href="toc.ncx"></item>
 <item id="Adventure1" media-type="text/x-oeb1-document" href="Adventure1.html"></item>
 <item id="Adventure2" media-type="text/x-oeb1-document" href="Adventure2.html"></item>
 <item id="Adventure3" media-type="text/x-oeb1-document" href="Adventure3.html"></item>
 <item id="Adventure4" media-type="text/x-oeb1-document" href="Adventure4.html"></item>
 <item id="Adventure5" media-type="text/x-oeb1-document" href="Adventure5.html"></item>
 <item id="Adventure6" media-type="text/x-oeb1-document" href="Adventure6.html"></item>
 <item id="Adventure7" media-type="text/x-oeb1-document" href="Adventure7.html"></item>
 <item id="Adventure8" media-type="text/x-oeb1-document" href="Adventure8.html"></item>
 <item id="Adventure9" media-type="text/x-oeb1-document" href="Adventure9.html"></item>
 <item id="Adventure10" media-type="text/x-oeb1-document" href="Adventure10.html"></item>
 <item id="Adventure11" media-type="text/x-oeb1-document" href="Adventure11.html"></item>
 <item id="Adventure12" media-type="text/x-oeb1-document" href="Adventure12.html"></item>
 <item id="SH_cover" href="cover.png" media-type="image/png"></item>
 <item id="Ch_start_image" href="Holmes_with_glass.png" media-type="image/png"></item>
</manifest>
```

We also need to add the spine to show the running order for the chapters as shown below:

```
<spine toc="ncx">
 <itemref idref="Adventure1"/>
 <itemref idref="Adventure2"/>
```

```
<itemref idref="Adventure3"/>
<itemref idref="Adventure4"/>
<itemref idref="Adventure5"/>
<itemref idref="Adventure6"/>
<itemref idref="Adventure7"/>
<itemref idref="Adventure8"/>
<itemref idref="Adventure9"/>
<itemref idref="Adventure10"/>
<itemref idref="Adventure11"/>
<itemref idref="Adventure12"/>
</spine>
```

Finally we need to add an element guide. With this element we are stating that the file toc.HTML has the title 'Table of Contents' and this is a reference of type 'toc'.

```
<guide>
<reference type="toc" title="Table of Contents" href="toc.html"/>
</guide>
```

We can now save all our work and compile the book. We have saved the OPF file as sherlockholmes.opf. Open a command prompt window and enter 'kindlegen sherlockholmes.opf' to create the book.

7 TUTORIAL 2 - CREATING A CHILDREN'S BOOK WITH KINDLE FORMAT 8

For this tutorial we will use the nursery rhyme, Old McDonald and create a simple but colourful eBook.

The Tutorial will show you how to:

•Adding a background image

•Format the text

•Position graphics using CSS

•Create a cover

•Creating the book

SETUP

Old McDonald is one of those strange nursery rhymes that can be as long as you wish, just add more animals. We are going to have five verse and will need pictures of five animals. These five animals are a cow, a pig, a horse, a dog and a duck. Create a folder called images and add the graphics to this. It is important to check the copyright information for any graphic file and only use those which you are allowed to use.

Start by creating a directory for the book. In this we will add the following:

•Three HTML files which are the pages of the book.

•Style.CSS

•Old McDonald.opf

The three blank HTML files should be called page01.html, page02.html and page03.html. For each of these files you should add the following content:

```
<head>
<title>Old McDonald Had A Farm</title>
<link rel="stylesheet" href="style.CSS" type="text/CSS"/>
</head>
<body>
</body>
</html>
```

In the header section the title is set as "Old McDonald Had A Farm" and it states that this file will use the stylesheet, style.CSS. The content will be placed between the opening body element and closing body element and there is no content here to start with.

The blank stylesheet should just have the following content:

```
<style type="text/CSS">
<!--


-->
</style>
```

The style information will be inserted between the third line from the top and third line from the bottom.

Add the following content to the OPF file to create a basic template which we will add to in this project:

```
<?xml version="1.0" encoding="UTF-8"?>
<package        xmlns:xx="http://saxon.sf.net/"        xmlns:atom="http://www.w3.org/2005/Atom"
xmlns:dc="http://purl.org/metadata/dublin_core" unique-identifier="BookId" version="2.0">
  <metadata xmlns:dc="http://purl.org/dc/elements/1.1/" xmlns:opf="http://www.idpf.org/2007/opf">

  </metadata>
  <manifest>
  <item id="stylesheet" href="style.CSS" media-type="text/CSS"/>
```

```
</manifest>
<spine toc="ncx">

</spine>
</package>
```

The OPF file is an XML file the root element is the package and this has three elements:

•Metadata is where the meta information about the book is held such as author, title etc.

•Manifest is the list of files used in the book.

•Spine is the order for the pages.

PAGE ORIENTATION

We want the book to be in landscape orientation and to have double pages on the Kindle screen. The first page will just have a picture of Old Mac Donald and a verse and picture on the facing page. The other HTML files will have the verse and picture on both pages.

In the OPF file we add the information that the book is in landscape by adding the following between the opening and closing <metadata> elements:

```
<meta name="fixed-layout" content="true"/>
<meta name="orientation-lock" content="landscape"/>
<meta name="original-resolution" content="1024x600"/>
```

This tell the Kindle that the book is fixed-layout, in landscape orientation and the original resolution is 1024 x 600.

In the stylesheet we adding to following code so that the area we are using is 600px by 1024px:

```
div.fs {
height: 600px;
width: 1024px;
position: relative;
}
```

We then add the following to identify the Left side (div.leftPage) and the right side (div.rightPage).

```
div.leftPage {
position: absolute;
background-repeat: no-repeat;
height: 600px;
width: 512px;
}


div.rightPage
{
position: absolute;
background-repeat: no-repeat;
height: 600px;
width: 512px;
left: 512px;
}
```

We will also add a background image in the stylesheet. As we want to make the book look like it is written on old paper we will use an image of an old book as the background. We have found an image which looks like old paper. We use the CSS element 'background-image'. This allows us to specify what the background image is.

```
#txtbg-img
{
background-image: url("images/Text-BG.jpg");
}
```

We then open the HTML files and add the opening <div class="fs"> element and the closing all element </div>.

This tells the HTML page that the 1024 x 600 resolution specified in the stylesheet is being used.

To add the background graphic for both the left and right side we add the following code:

```
<div id="txtbg-img" class="leftPage"></div>
 <div id="txtbg-img" class="rightPage"></div>
```

We then add the opening element <div class="leftPage"> and closing element </div>. All the content on the left hand side page will be placed between this. All the content on the right hand side will be placed the opening element, <div class="rightPage"> and the closing element, </div>.

Each of the three HTML pages should have exactly the same content at this stage.

FORMATTING AND ADDING THE TEXT

In this tutorial we are going to use the fonts which are already available on the Kindle Fire. In the chapter on Fonts in the How To section, I will provide greater information on fonts including how to specify a font and upload this as part of your KF8 file.

We specify the font we want as an extension of the body element. All the text you see on a page is within the body element so doing it this way ensures that we control the font throughout the book.

```
body
{
font-family: baskerville, Lucida;
font-size: 120%;<
}
```

The font-family attribute states which font is to be used. The page will use the first font in the list and if that is not there it will use the next list. Any number of fonts can be listed here but on a Kindle there are a relatively small number of fonts. In this case Baskerville is one of the fonts which are on a Kindle Fire so this will be used. If none of the fonts listed after the font-family attribute are present the Kindle will use the default font.

The font-size attribute states the characters will be 20% bigger than usual.

We want to position the text so that each verse is positioned 5% down the page and with an 11% margin. We are going to insert a graphic without a verse on the left hand side of page01.html and a graphic and the verse on the right hand side. With page02.html and page03.html we will insert a graphic and verse on both the left and right hand sides.

To do this we add the following code to the stylesheet:

```
.postext
{
position:absolute;
top: 5%;
left: 11%;
}
```

We then open page01.html and go to element <div class="rightPage"> and after this we insert the verse. This text should be inserted between an opening element, <div class="postext">, and a closing </div> element. This should look as follows:

<div class="postext">Old Macdonald had a farm, E-I-E-I-O

And on his farm he had a cow, E-I-E-I-O

With a "moo-moo" here and a "moo-moo" there

Here a "moo" there a "moo"

Everywhere a "moo-moo"

Old Macdonald had a farm, E-I-E-I-O</div>

We then insert the second verse on the left hand side of page02.html and the third verse on the right hand side. The fourth verse goes on the left hand side of page03.html and the fifth verse goes on the right hand side.

POSITION GRAPHICS USING CSS

We are going to position all the graphics in the same position on each page. We do this by creating some CSS code which will position the graphic where we want it.

We place a picture of Old McDonald on the first page of the book. As we do not put text here we use different values for the top and left position as shown below.

```
.pos1stimg
{
position:absolute;
top: 20%;
left: 15%;
}
```

The position attribute has the value 'absolute'. This means the graphic will be positioned in an exact place. The attribute 'top' has a percentage value and in this case the graphic will be positioned so that the top is 20% of the way down the page. The 'left' attribute positions the graphic 15% to the left of the page.

To position this graphic we open page01.html and insert the following code after the element, <div class="leftPage">:

<div class="pos1stimg">

```
<img src="images/oldmacdonald.gif" />
</div>
```

For each page with a verse we use the following CSS code to position the image.

```
.posimg
{
position:absolute;
top: 39%;
left: 11%;
}
```

In each of the HTML files we go to where we have placed the text for the verse and insert an appropriate picture using the following code:

```
<div class="posimg">
<img src="images/cow.gif" style="float-offset:left">
</div>
```

The picture below each verse should be of the animal mentioned in the verse.

CREATE A COVER

It is mandatory to have a cover which is used for marketing purposes on the Amazon website and for the book. These should be the same image but it is possible to use different files for them.

The cover we are using is a GIF file where we have added the text "Old McDonald" to his picture. This image is 1394 by 1528 Pixels. Amazon specify that the longest side should be between 1000 and 2500 Pixels and the shortest side should be more than 500 Pixels.

I have named the file cover.gif. I add the following entry in the metadata section of the opf file <meta name="cover" content="my_cover_image" />.

This states that I have used "my_cover_image" as the ID for the cover.

In the manifest section I add

```
<item id="my_cover_image" href="images/cover.gif" media-type="image/gif"/>
```

This states the item with the id "my_cover_image" is a GIF file and where it can be found.

BUILDING THE BOOK

At this stage the HTML pages and stylesheet are complete but we need to complete the OPF file before compiling the book.

In the metadata section we will add the following lines

```
<meta name="book-type" content="children"/>
<meta name="RegionMagnification" content="true"/>
```

The first line states the book is for children and the second states that it is possible to magnify a portion of the text. Amazon require this for Children's books.

We will now add information about the title and author of the book.

```
<dc-metadata                          xmlns:dc="http://purl.org/metadata/dublin_core"
xmlns:oebpackage="http://openbook.org/namespaces/oeb-package/1.0/">
<dc:title>Old McDonald</dc:title>
<dc:language>en</dc:language>
<dc:creator>Nursery Rhyme</dc:creator>
</dc-metadata>
```

This uses the Dublin Core which is a standard for metadata which describes a document. The use of the prefix 'dc:' specifies that it is a Dublin Core element. Here the title, language and creator are specified.

In the manifest section we must specify the items which are used in this book. To do this we add the following code:

```
<item id="stylesheet" href="style.CSS" media-type="text/CSS"/>
<item id="page01" href="page01.html" media-type="application/xhtml+xml"/>
<item id="page02" href="page02.html" media-type="application/xhtml+xml"/>
<item id="page03" href="page03.html" media-type="application/xhtml+xml"/>
<!-- images -->
<item id="my_cover_image" href="images/cover.gif" media-type="image/gif"/>
<item id="textbackground" href="images/Text-BG.jpg" media-type="image/jpeg"/>
```

```
<item id="cowimg" href="images/cow.gif" media-type="image/gif"/>
<item id="pigimg" href="images/pig.gif" media-type="image/gif"/>
<item id="dogimg" href="images/dog.gif" media-type="image/gif"/>
<item id="horseimg" href="images/horse.gif" media-type="image/gif"/>
<item id="duckimg" href="images/duck.gif" media-type="image/gif"/>
 </manifest>
```

Each of the item elements have an id which will be used in the spine section that follows, a href value which states the location of a the file to be used and a media-type attribute which states what sort of file it is.

The final section of the OPF file is the spine. Here we list the files in the order they will appear in the book:

```
<spine> <itemref idref="page01"/>
<itemref idref="page02"/>
<itemref idref="page03"/>
</spine>
```

We now save all our files and open a command prompt window for the folder we are using. Our OPF file was labelled 'Old McDonald.opf'. If we just typed the text 'kindlegen Old McDonald.opf' we would get an error message stating the file 'McDonald.opf' could not found. This is because of the spaces in the file name. We simply insert the filename between a set of double quotes as in the following 'kindlegen "Old McDonald.opf"'.

Our book is now compiled and ready for reading in a Kindle device.

8 MORE FORMATTING TECHNIQUES

CSS

It is a good habit to make your formatting changes in CSS. This means that if you want to make a change to the formatting you make one change in your CSS file rather than hundreds of changes in your HTML file. You have already seen how we changed the way paragraphs appear in the text. The alternative to a few lines in the CSS file instructing the paragraphs to be indented and justified is to make this change to each and every <p> element in the HTML files.

@media

Amazon allows you to use more than one CSS style-sheet in your eBook. The device will then choose the correct CSS style-sheet. This is achieved by using the @media function in CSS.

If you have two sets of CSS code such as that written below:

```
@media="amzn-kf8"
{
// Code for Amazon Kindle Format 8


}
```

and

```
@media="amzn-mobi"
{
// Code for Amazon mobi
}
```

The code in @media="amzn-kf8"section will be executed if the devises uses Kindle Format 8 and the code in@media="amzn-mobi"section will be executed if the devises uses Amazon mobi. However, most Kindles now support Kindle Format 8.

P Justify

You can justify the text in a paragraph by using the command text-align:justify

If you put the following code in your CSS file:

p { text-align:justify;}

the text in your HTML document between the <p> and </p> will be justified.

P Indent

You can justify the indent the first line in a paragraph by using the command text-indent:50px;}

If you put the following code in your CSS file:

p {text-indent:50px;}

the text in your HTML document between the <p> and </p> will be indented by 50 px.

You can also use several command together by putting the following code in your CSS file:

p { text-align:justify; text-indent:50px;}

the paragraph will be both justified and the first line indented by 50 px.

P Font

CSS uses a period after an element to define a class of that element.

For example the following code in your CSS file:

p.serif{font-family:"Times New Roman",Times,serif;}

p.sansserif{font-family:Arial,Helvetica,sans-serif;}

define two classes of the element <p> and the font-family lists the fonts to be used. If the first font is not available it will use the second font and if this is not available the third. If none are available it will use the default font.

The following is how this would appear in the HTML document.

<p class="serif">This is a paragraph, shown in the Times New Roman font.</p>

<p class="sansserif">This is a paragraph, shown in the Arial font.</p>

It is also possible to use other font specification such as font-size, font-style, font-boldness etc.

I usually do not specify the font for eBooks and leave it to the device to decide on this.

Drop caps

One effect which was introduced with Kindle Format 8 and EPUB version is the ability to have drop capitals

If you use the following code in your CSS file:

```
@media="amzn-kf8"
{
span.dropcapsA
{
float: left;
font-size: 4em;
font-weight: bold;
color:#000000;
margin-top: -.2em;
margin-bottom: -.2em;
margin-right: .1em;
padding-right: .1em;
text-shadow:5px -3px #151B54;
}
}


@media="amzn-mobi"
{
```

```
span.dropcapsA

{

font-size: xx-large;

font-weight: bold;

color: #C11B17;

}

}
```

and use the following in you your HTML document:

```
<span class="dropcapsA">One</span> Two Three
```

The word "One" will appear as drop capital in a device which supports Kindle Format 8 and a larger bold font in a device which doesn't.

Headings

The tags <h1> to <h6> are used for the six level of heading available in HTML. It is possible to use CSS to extend the format of the <h1> to <h6> elements.

In CSS you can add attributes which change the text, font, color of the heading element. For example the following code in a CSS file:

```
h1

{

color:red;

text-align:center;

font-family:"Times New Roman";

}
```

Will cause the text in between the start and end h1 element in the HTML document to be red, aligned centrally and use the Times New Roman font.

div

The div element defines a division with HTML. For example the following code in a CSS file would define a class called "redbox":

div.redbox

{

width:220px;

padding:10px;

border:5px solid red;

margin:0px;

}

When you called this class in HTML with the following code:

<div class="redbox">The is a box with a red border.</div>

You will get a box as specified in the CSS file.

Position images

The div element can also be used to position images in a HTML file. In the second tutorial for the Kindle Format 8 we will create a book have landscape orientation and be divided in two as if we were looking at landscape screen divided into two pages.

Dividing the screen into two is achieved by two div classes:

```
div.leftPage {
position: absolute;
background-repeat: no-repeat;
height: 600px;
width: 512px; /* Half the fixed spread width */
```

```
}
```

```
div.rightPage {
position: absolute;
background-repeat: no-repeat;
height: 600px;
width: 512px;
left: 512px;
}
```

and the following code in the CSS is used for the background image:

```
#txtbg-img
{
background-image: url("images/Text-BG.jpg");
}
```

There is an image Text-BG.jpg located in the images directory.

In the HTML file we only need the following code:

```
<div id="txtbg-img" class="leftPage"></div>
<div id="txtbg-img" class="rightPage"></div>
```

Borders

Border are another interesting effect which can achieved using CSS and HTML. For example the following code in a CSS file:

```
p.brd

{

border-style:solid;

border-width:10px;
```

```
border-color:red;


}
```

and the following code in the HTML document:

```
<p class="brd">Border example</p>
```

would show a solid red border of 10 px round this text.

Body text

You should not change the body text within a document. This will cause problems with different devices which may not have a particular font or the user may want the text to appear in a certain way.

Amazon states that the body should be default and give the following guidelines:

•Body text must not have a forced alignment (such as left aligned or justified).

•Body text must use the default font size. Body text should not use the <font size=""> tag or its equivalent in CSS.

•Body text should not be bold or italicized. Selected parts of the text can be bold or italicized. This guideline only prohibits a book that would be entirely bold, for example.

•Body text should not have an imposed font color.

•Body text must not have a white font color. Customers report this as a bad user experience.

•Body text must not have a black background color. Customers report this as a bad user experience.

Page numbers

You should not use page numbers in your eBook as different devices will have different page numbers for the same section. If you would like to reference something in the text simply insert a hyperlink to it.

Add the code <a name="intsec">Interesting section</a> to the place where you want the link to go to and insert the following code in the place where you want the hyperlink to be: <a href="content.html#intsec">This is an interesting section</a>

content.html is the HTML where the section you want the link to go to is. If both sections are in the same file you just #intsec rather than content.html#intsec

Fixed Layout books

Tutorial 2 provides an example of fixed layout book. I would use this technique sparingly and make sure that the contents needs this sort of approach before doing this.

Special characters and Unicode

Amazon Kindle uses Unicode as its default code page. However you should not use Unicode Format Characters within the text. These are invisible characters used to do something t the appearance of neighbouring characters.

Back Cover

The use of back covers is something which Amazon suggests could be useful with children's books. It was not done previously. A back cover would be a HTML page similar to a physical book's back cover.

Audio and Video

Note: At the time of writing this is only supported on the Kindle app on an iPad. There is an additional problem with Kindle eBooks which are added to your iPad through iTunes. These do not find the audio or video file to play. This section is added as Amazon have documented the use of audio in their guidelines for creating Kindle files and are likely to introduce this functionality in Kindle devices in the near future. You can see more information in the how to sections below.

HTML 5 has seen the introduction of two new multimedia elements <audio> and <video>.

Kindle Format 8 allows you to embed audio but not to stream it. Amazon recommends using stereo channels in the MP3 source as the Kindle device supports playback in stereo.

Insert Tables

You should be very careful about inserting tables with an eBook. The problem is that what appears in Word as a perfectly defined table may look awful in the Kindle.

It would be a good idea to use media queries so that a table is only displayed in a Kindle Format 8 document as tables do not work very on older Kindle devices.

Page breaks

Amazon state you should use the CSS attribute page-break-before and page-break-after to insert a page break

If you have the code

```
h1 {page-break-before:always}
```

you will always have a page break before the <h1> heading.

W3schools.com

I would strongly recommend you learning some more about CSS as if you are doing much formatting in your eBooks this will be extremely helpful. One of the best sources of tutorials and information on this is the W3 Schools http://www.w3schools.com/. They have a very cool feature on their site which allows you to try for yourself.

9 THE EPUB FORMAT

EPUB is an open source industry standard for eBooks. Most eReaders other than the Kindle use this format including the Barnes and Noble Nook and iPad and Android devices. Amazon's mobi and Kindle format 8 are based on the EPUB format.

The intention in this book is to concentrate on the Kindle Format 8 but to give an introduction to the EPUB format. In the resources section there is a list of websites where you can get more valuable information.

EPUB is a compressed ZIP format with the extension .epub. If you changed the extension of an EPUB file from .epub to .zip you would be able to uncompress it and examine the files and structure.

EPUB VERSION 3

EPUB version 3 was published in October 2011. It is a major upgrade from EPUB 2.0.

There were a number of issues which EPUB 3 addresses and it is a significant improvement on previous versions. EPUB 2 was seen as very useful for text centric books but unsuitable for eBooks which require media, precise layout or specialised formatting. It makes use of functionality which has become available with HTML 5. The problem that technical publications had with EPUB 2's lack of support for MathML has been addressed in EPUB 3. This standard also address the specification's lack of detail on linking into, between, or within an EPUB book, and its lack of a specification for annotation.

EPUB 3 consists of a set of four specifications:

- EPUB Publications 3.0, which defines publication-level semantics and overarching conformance requirements for EPUB Publications

- EPUB Content Documents 3.0, which defines profiles of XHTML, SVG and CSS for use in the context of EPUB Publications

- EPUB Open Container Format (OCF) 3.0, which defines a file format and processing model for encapsulating a set of related resources into a single-file (ZIP) EPUB Container.

- EPUB Media Overlays 3.0, which defines a format and a processing model for synchronization of text and audio

EPUB Publications 3.0

This document defines the publication publication-level semantics and conformance requirements for EPUB® 3. It also defines the rules and format for the package document.

The package document contains the following sections:

- Package element - This is the required main xml element for the file.

- Metadata element - This is a required element where the metadata about the book is listed.

- Manifest element - This required element is where all the documents and other resources which make up the eBook are listed.

- Spine - This required element defines the default reading order of the eBook.

- Guide element - This element was used in EPUB 2 but is deprecated in EPUB 3. You should use the landmarks feature in the EPUB Navigation Document.

- Bindings element - This optional element defines a set of custom handlers for media types not supported by this specification.

The full specification for EPUB Publications 3.0 is available here: http://www.idpf.org/EPUB/30/spec/EPUB30-publications.html

EPUB Content Documents 3.0

This document defines how EPUB uses HTML5, CSS and SVG. EPUB 3 uses a XHTML document which is based on HTML 5. EPUB readers are not expected to support all HML5 features such as scripting, HTML5 forms or HTML5 DOM. CSS in EPUB uses CSS 2.1 as its baseline and any document which conforms to CSS 2.1 should work in EPUB. EPUB uses a restricted subset of SVG 1.1.

The full specification for EPUB Content Documents 3.0 is available here: http://www.idpf.org/EPUB/30/spec/EPUB30-contentdocs.html

EPUB Open Container Format (OCF) 3.0

This document specifies the container file where the EPUB publications are stored.

The full specification for EPUB Open Container Format (OCF) 3.0 is available here: http://www.idpf.org/EPUB/30/spec/EPUB30-ocf.html

EPUB Media Overlays 3.0

EPUB 3 specifies a subset of SMIL (Synchronized Multimedia Integration Language) to provide synchronisation of media files within an eBook.

The full specification for EPUB EPUB Media Overlays 3.0 is available here: http://www.idpf.org/EPUB/30/spec/EPUB30-mediaoverlays.html

Tutorials

In the next two chapters we have two tutorial. In the first we will be creating an EPUB 2.0 eBook and in the second we will converting this eBook to EPUB 3.0. This should be seen as just an introduction to this standard and I would highly recommend you using the resources listed at the end of this book to discover more about the EPUB format.

10 TUTORIAL 3 - CREATING AN EPUB EBOOK

We will use Sir Arthur Conan Doyle's collection of short stories, The Adventures of Sherlock Holmes, for our tutorial. This book and many other classics which are out of copyright are available for Project Guttenberg www.gutenberg.net

The Tutorial will show you how to do the following:

- Convert a book from text to HTML in your word processor

- Formatting the Chapters

- Structure the book

- Add a cover

- Add metadata

- Add illustrations

- Building an EPUB eBook

- Validating the EPUB book

FILE STRUCTURE

The EPUB file container is a zip file with a specific structure which is understood by EPUB readers.

In the root of the container is a single mimetype file and two directories, one called META-INF/ and the other is usually called OEBPS/ but can be called something else.

The mimetype file contains the text, " application/EPUB+zip " and nothing more.

The META-INF/ directory must contain file called "container.xml" but can also contain the following optional files manifest.xml, metadata.xml, signatures.xml, encryption.xml and rights.xml.

In this tutorial we will use only the container.xml.

We will use a file called sherlock.opf as our package file and the container.xml which show where that file is to be found.

The container.xml will have the following content.

```
<?xml version="1.0"?>
<container version="1.0" xmlns="urn:oasis:names:tc:opendocument:xmlns:container">
<rootfiles>
<rootfile full-path="OEBPS/sherlock.opf"
media-type="application/oebps-package+xml" />
</rootfiles>
</container>
```

The element rootfile shows that sherlock.opf is located in the OEBPS directory.

In the OEBPS directory we will have one directory for images and all other files in the OEBPS directory.

One of the common problems which occur when you first start working with EPUB is not being able to zip the file correctly. EPUB expects the first file in the container to be the mimetype and if you use Windows compression or many other compression utilities they will compress the file so that the directories are before the mimetype file. To make matters worse when you try and validate your EPUB book you will get an error which states the validator expect 8 characters in the name of the first file but found 22. Not the most informative of errors.

I use a utility called ePubPack http://sourceforge.net/projects/epubpack/. This is a freeware utility which zips the EPUB container correctly.

THE CONTENT

We will again use the The Aventures of Sherlock Holmes for our eBook. As described in Tutorial 1 I have used the search and replace to add opening paragraph marks <p> and closing paragraph marks </p> and the beginning and end of each paragraph.

We then create twelve HTML files which are labeled Adventure1.html, Adventure2.html and so on and add the following text to each of them.

```
<!DOCTYPE html>
<html xmlns="http://www.w3.org/1999/xhtml">
<head>
<title>The Adventures of Sherlock Holmes</title>
<link type="text/CSS" href="styles.CSS" rel="Stylesheet"/>
</head>
```

```
<body>

</body>
</html>
```

I then copy each of the chapter into the appropriate HTML file. I make sure that all the pagraphs in each story are between <p> and </p> elements.

FORMATTING THE CHAPTERS

We want the chapters formatted with the title of the adventure in large text with a silhouette of Sherlock Holmes below it. Most of the text will formatted by simply inserting it between a start and end paragraph mark. The first sentence in each chapter will use drop capitals.

Open adventure1.html in my HTML editor. In the header of this and the other chapters there is an element title. This is the HTML element which gives a browser the title of the page you are viewing. Some Kindle devices also display this text. I will use the name of the book rather than the chapter name here and I copy "The Adventures of Sherlock Holmes" between the start and end <title> elements.

I shall put the title of the story with <h1> elements. This is equivalent to Heading 1 in Microsoft Word. I will use <h1> for the names of the stories and <h2> if there chapters within one of the stories. One advantage of using CSS is that if at any stage I want to change how the chapter titles are displayed I just have to make one change to how the <h1> element is specified in the CSS file and it will format all titles the same way.

I have also adding a graphic with a silhouette of Holmes after each title and split the title so that the number of the story is in the first line and the actual title starts on the second.

The code for this is as follows:

```
<h1>ADVENTURE I. <br/>A SCANDAL IN BOHEMIA</h1>
<p> </p>
<p><img src="images/Holmes_with_glass.png" alt="Sherlock Holmes" </p>
<h2>I.</h2>
```

The <h1> element which is used for the title is split by the line break element <br/>. The image is inserted using the HTML editor wizard for adding an image. This looks after the size etc. However, with the Kindle you could just leave out everything other than <img src="images/Holmes_with_glass.png">. I have added an alt="Sherlock Holmes" attribute here as it is required that you use an alt attribute

The <h2> element is used to highlight the subsections in some of these stories.

CSS FILE

I want the heading to be formatted a bit differently to the way they usually appear. I achieved this through the CSS. In this I add the code:

```
h1 {
font-size: 1.5em;
line-height: 1.33em;
text-align: center;
padding-bottom: 0em;
text-align: center;
text-transform: uppercase;
font-weight: normal;
letter-spacing: 4px;
}
```

and

```
h2 {
text-align: center;
font-size: 1.33em;
line-height: 1.2em;
text-align: center;
padding-bottom: 0em;
text-align: center;
text-transform: uppercase;
font-weight: normal;
letter-spacing: 3px;
}
```

With both <h1> and <h2> the headings will be centered, upper case and bigger than usual with more space between the letter. The main difference is that <h1> will have a bigger text size than <h2>

I also want each paragraph to be indented by 50 px and justified. I do this by adding the following code:

```
p {
text-indent:50px;
text-align: justify;
}
```

I call my file styles.CSS and locate this in the OEBPS directory. I have already added the declaration for this CSS file to the HTML files:

```
<link type="text/CSS" href="styles.CSS" rel="Stylesheet"/>
```

and the elements I use (<p>, <h1> and <h2>) are already in the HTML document so there is no need to change anything further. The EPUB reader will show the book the way I want it.

ADD A COVER

One area where EPUB differs from the Kindle is that you need a cover HTML file for an EPUB file. With the Kindle you upload the cover as an image file separately and Amazon attaches it to your book. I will user the cover.png file we created in Tutorial 1 and simply add this to a file.

I create a HTML and add the image as shown below:

```
<?xml version="1.0" encoding="UTF-8"?><html xmlns="http://www.w3.org/1999/xhtml"
xmlns:EPUB="http://www.idpf.org/2007/ops">
  <head>
  <title>The Adventures of Sherlock Holmes</title>
  <link rel="stylesheet" type="text/CSS" href="styles.CSS"/>
  </head>
  <body>
  <p> <img src="images/cover.png" alt="Cover Image" title="Cover Image"/> </p>
  </body>
  </html>
```

STRUCTURE THE BOOK

We will use an OPF to provide the structure of the book and an NCX and HTML file to provide the navigation and table of contents for the book. We will start our work on the OPF file.

The first element in the package file is the <package> element.

```
<package xmlns="http://www.idpf.org/2007/opf" unique-identifier="SholmeskId" version="2.0">
```

This shows the namespace for EPUB 2, an identifier and the version of EPUB we are using. In this case it is 2.0

Add metadata

In the metadata section we will add the title of the book, the author and the language. All of these use Dublin Core metadata terms. EPUB differs from Kindle Format 8 in that you must add an identifier for the book here. This is usually the ISBN number but can be any unique identifier,

The first <metadata> element tell where the namespace for the Dublin Core can be found.

We add the title by inserting the text between <dc:title> opening and closing tags.

```
<dc:title id="title">The Adventures of Sherlock Holmes</dc:title>
```

We will add the name of the author:

```
<dc:creator id="creator">Sir Arthur Conan Doyle</dc:creator>
```

We will add an ID. As we have not got an ISBN number for this tutorial we will use a namespace:

```
<dc:identifier id="SholmeskId">EPUBservicesco.com.sherlock-holmes</dc:identifier>
```

In order to specify the language we use the ISO 639 language codes. Each language is given a code which will be universally understood by a machine processing the text. In this case the language is English so we use the code 'en'. Language codes are always written in lower case.

```
<dc:language>en</dc:language>
```

The final element we add is a refence to the cover which does not use the Dublin Core.

```
<meta name="cover" content="cover.png" />
```

The complete code for the metadata section is as follows:

```
<metadata xmlns:dc="http://purl.org/dc/elements/1.1/">
 <dc:title id="title">The Adventures of Sherlock Holmes</dc:title>
 <dc:creator id="creator">Sir Arthur Conan Doyle</dc:creator>
 <dc:identifier id="SholmeskId">EPUBservicesco.com.sherlock-holmes</dc:identifier>
 <dc:language>en</dc:language>
  <meta name="cover" content="cover.png" />

</metadata>
```

MANIFEST

In the manifest section we want to add all the files were using. This includes all the HTML files, images, style sheet. If we were adding a font to the EPUB container we would mention it here.

The code below shows how this is done:

```
<manifest>
  <item id="style" href="styles.CSS" media-type="text/CSS"/>
  <item id="content" media-type="application/xhtml+xml" href="toc.html"></item>
  <item id="ncx" media-type="application/x-dtbncx+xml" href="toc.ncx"></item>
  <item id="Adventure1" media-type="application/xhtml+xml" href="adventure1.html"></item>
  <item id="Adventure2" media-type="application/xhtml+xml" href="adventure2.html"></item>
  <item id="Adventure3" media-type="application/xhtml+xml" href="adventure3.html"></item>
  <item id="Adventure4" media-type="application/xhtml+xml" href="adventure4.html"></item>
  <item id="Adventure5" media-type="application/xhtml+xml" href="adventure5.html"></item>
  <item id="Adventure6" media-type="application/xhtml+xml" href="adventure6.html"></item>
  <item id="Adventure7" media-type="application/xhtml+xml" href="adventure7.html"></item>
  <item id="Adventure8" media-type="application/xhtml+xml" href="adventure8.html"></item>
  <item id="Adventure9" media-type="application/xhtml+xml" href="adventure9.html"></item>
  <item id="Adventure10" media-type="application/xhtml+xml" href="adventure10.html"></item>
  <item id="Adventure11" media-type="application/xhtml+xml" href="adventure11.html"></item>
  <item id="Adventure12" media-type="application/xhtml+xml" href="adventure12.html"></item>
  <item id="cover.xhtml" media-type="application/xhtml+xml" href="cover.xhtml"/>
  <item id="SH_cover" href="images/cover.png" media-type="image/png"></item>
  <item id="Ch_start_image" href="images/Holmes_with_glass.png" media-type="image/png"></item>
</manifest>
```

TABLE OF CONTENTS

When using a Table of Contents in a Kindle book you need two Table of contents files. toc.HTML is a HTML file and toc.ncx is an XML navigation file.

To create the toc.HTML we have the name of the book in a H1 element and an ordered list with links to each chapter in the order they appear and each link has the name of the chapter. This is shown below:

```
<ul>
```

```
<li><a href="adventure1.html">ADVENTURE I. A SCANDAL IN BOHEMIA</a></li>

<li><a href="adventure2.html">ADVENTURE II. THE RED-HEADED LEAGUE</a></li>

<li><a href="adventure3.html">ADVENTURE III. A CASE OF IDENTITY</a></li>

<li><a href="adventure4.html">ADVENTURE IV. THE BOSCOMBE VALLEY MYSTERY</a></li>

<li><a href="adventure5.html">ADVENTURE V. THE FIVE ORANGE PIPS</a></li>

<li><a href="adventure6.html">ADVENTURE VI. THE MAN WITH THE TWISTED LIP</a></li>

<li><a href="adventure7.html">ADVENTURE VII. THE ADVENTURE OF THE BLUE CARBUNCLE</a></li>

<li><a href="adventure8.html">ADVENTURE VIII. THE ADVENTURE OF THE SPECKLED BAND</a></li>

<li><a href="adventure9.html">ADVENTURE IX. THE ADVENTURE OF THE ENGINEER'S THUMB</a></li>

<li><a href="adventure10.html">ADVENTURE X. THE ADVENTURE OF THE NOBLE BACHELOR</a></li>

<li><a href="adventure11.html">ADVENTURE XI. THE ADVENTURE OF THE BERYL CORONET</a></li>

<li><a href="adventure12.html">ADVENTURE XII. THE ADVENTURE OF THE COPPER BEECHES</a></li>

</ul>
```

To create the toc.ncx we add a navMap which a serious of naPoints. These tool us the order they appea and the navLabel gives us the text which is used. See below:

```
<navMap>
    <navPoint id="navpoint-1" playOrder="1"><navLabel><text>ADVENTURE I. A SCANDAL IN BOHEMIA</text></navLabel><content src="adventure1.html"/></navPoint>

    <navPoint id="navpoint-2" playOrder="2"><navLabel><text>ADVENTURE II. THE RED-HEADED LEAGUE</text></navLabel><content src="adventure2.html"/></navPoint>

    <navPoint id="navpoint-3" playOrder="3"><navLabel><text>ADVENTURE III. A CASE OF IDENTITY</text></navLabel><content src="adventure3.html"/></navPoint>

    <navPoint id="navpoint-4" playOrder="4"><navLabel><text>ADVENTURE IV. THE BOSCOMBE VALLEY MYSTERY</text></navLabel><content src="adventure4.html"/></navPoint>

    <navPoint id="navpoint-5" playOrder="5"><navLabel><text>ADVENTURE V. THE FIVE ORANGE PIPS</text></navLabel><content src="adventure5.html"/></navPoint>

    <navPoint id="navpoint-6" playOrder="6"><navLabel><text>ADVENTURE VI. THE MAN WITH THE TWISTED LIP</text></navLabel><content src="adventure6.html"/></navPoint>

    <navPoint id="navpoint-7" playOrder="7"><navLabel><text>ADVENTURE VII. THE ADVENTURE OF THE BLUE CARBUNCLE</text></navLabel><content src="adventure7.html"/></navPoint>

    <navPoint id="navpoint-8" playOrder="8"><navLabel><text>ADVENTURE VIII. THE ADVENTURE OF THE SPECKLED BAND</text></navLabel><content src="adventure8.html"/></navPoint>

    <navPoint id="navpoint-9" playOrder="9"><navLabel><text>ADVENTURE IX. THE ADVENTURE OF THE ENGINEER'S THUMB</text></navLabel><content src="adventure9.html"/></navPoint>
```

<navPoint id="navpoint-10" playOrder="10"><navLabel><text>ADVENTURE X. THE ADVENTURE OF THE NOBLE BACHELOR</text></navLabel><content sr="adventure0.html"/></navPoint>

<navPoint id="navpoint-11" playOrder="11"><navLabel><text>ADVENTURE XI. THE ADVENTURE OF THE BERYL CORONET</text></navLabel><content src="adventure11.html"/></navPoint>

<navPoint id="navpoint-12" playOrder="12"><navLabel><text>ADVENTURE XII. THE ADVENTURE OF THE COPPER BEECHES</text></navLabel><content src="adventure12.html"/></navPoint>

</navMap>

Completing the OPF file and building the book

At this stage we should have 12 HTML files, 2 image files, a toc.HTML file, a toc.ncx and a stylesheet, style.CSS.

We also need to add the spine to show the running order for the chapters as shown below:

<spine toc="ncx">
  <itemref idref="cover.xhtml"/>
  <itemref idref="Adventure1"/>
  <itemref idref="Adventure2"/>
  <itemref idref="Adventure3"/>
  <itemref idref="Adventure4"/>
  <itemref idref="Adventure5"/>
  <itemref idref="Adventure6"/>
  <itemref idref="Adventure7"/>
  <itemref idref="Adventure8"/>
  <itemref idref="Adventure9"/>
  <itemref idref="Adventure10"/>
  <itemref idref="Adventure11"/>
  <itemref idref="Adventure12"/>
  </spine>

Finally we need to add an element guide. With this element we are stating that the file toc.HTML has the title 'Table of Contents' and this is a reference of type 'toc'.

<guide>
  <reference type="toc" title="Table of Contents" href="toc.html"/>
  </guide>

We can now save all our work and build the book. The file structure should be as follows:

mimetype

META-INF\container.xml

OEBPS\images\cover.png

OEBPS\images\Holmes_with_glass.png

OEBPS\adventure1.html

OEBPS\adventure10.html

OEBPS\adventure11.html

OEBPS\adventure12.html

OEBPS\adventure2.html

OEBPS\adventure3.html

OEBPS\adventure4.html

OEBPS\adventure5.html

OEBPS\adventure6.html

OEBPS\adventure7.html

OEBPS\adventure8.html

OEBPS\adventure9.html

OEBPS\cover.xhtml

OEBPS\sherlock.opf

OEBPS\styles.CSS

OEBPS\toc.html

OEBPS\toc.ncx

Validating the EPUB file

Building the file with a compression tool like EPUBPack should result in valid EPUB file.

However this will not always be the case. I use the Java EPUB validation tool ePubcheck-3.0.1.jar. This is available at: http://code.google.com/p/epubcheck/ There is also information available on the errors which you find with this tool: http://code.google.com/p/epubcheck/wiki/Errors You will also find comments from other users which are extremely useful.

11 TUTORIAL 4 CONVERTING THE EPUB 2 BOOK TO EPUB 3

In this tutorial we will take the EPUB 2 book which we have just built and convert it to EPUB 3.

The tutorial cover:

- Differences between EPUB 2 and EPUB 3
- Changes to the navigation
- Changes to the OPF file

DIFFERENCES BETWEEN EPUB 2 AND EPUB 3

The most substantial differences between EPUB 2 and EPUB 3 relate to changes brought in through HTML5. The use of audio, video and greater support for non-text based books such as technical manuals using MathML are some of the major changes with EPUB 3. This tutorial will not deal with these but in the reference section I list some websites where you can get further information.

HTML5 introduced a new element <nav> to deal with navigation. EPUB3 has replaced the .ncx and HTML table of contents file with a single table of contents file which uses the <nav> element.

NAVIGATION

We are going to take the HTML table of contents we used in Tutorial 3 and convert this to an EPUB 3 table of contents file.

The root HTML element we used for the EPUB 2 project has got a reference to the XHTML namespace:

<html xmlns="http://www.w3.org/1999/xhtml">

We will change this to include the EPUB namespace:

<html xmlns="http://www.w3.org/1999/xhtml" xmlns:EPUB="http://www.idpf.org/2007/ops">

We will now add the <nav> element. The content of this file is a list of links to the chapters of our book and we want all of this to be between the start and end <nav> elements.

Just after the <body> element we insert the following:

<nav id="toc" EPUB:type="toc">

This gives the <nav> element the id "toc" and also the attribute EPUB:type="toc".

Just before the closing </body> element we will add the closing </nav> element.

In the EPUB 2 file the heading <h1> had the id "toc". As there is no need for that now, we will remove the attribute and just have the text: <h1>Table of Contents</h1>

We now have an ordered list with each list item similar to this:

<li>
 <a href="Adventure1.html">ADVENTURE I. A SCANDAL IN BOHEMIA</a>
 </li>

We will give each <li> element an attribute which identifies the chapter. This is the similar to the attributes used in the ncx file in EPUB 2. For each list item we add an id such as "adventure1", "adventure2" etc. as in:

<li id="Adventure1">
 <a href="Adventure1.html">ADVENTURE I. A SCANDAL IN BOHEMIA</a>
 </li>

We will add the cover as the first list item:

<li id="cover">
 <a href="cover.xhtml">Cover</a>
 </li>

We will call our file toc.xhtml and delete the old toc.ncx and toc.html files. The complete listing for the new file is:

<?xml version="1.0" encoding="UTF-8"?>
 <html xmlns="http://www.w3.org/1999/xhtml" xmlns:EPUB="http://www.idpf.org/2007/ops">

```
<head>
<title>TOC</title>
<link type="text/CSS" href="styles.CSS" rel="Stylesheet"/>
</head>
<body>
<nav id="toc" EPUB:type="toc">
<h1>Table of Contents</h1>

<ol>
<li id="cover">
<a href="cover.xhtml">Cover</a>
</li>
<li id="Adventure1">
<a href="Adventure1.html">ADVENTURE I. A SCANDAL IN BOHEMIA</a>
</li>
<li id="Adventure2">
<a href="Adventure2.html">ADVENTURE II. THE RED-HEADED LEAGUE</a>
</li>
<li id="Adventure3">
<a href="Adventure3.html">ADVENTURE III. A CASE OF IDENTITY</a>
</li>
<li id="Adventure4">
<a href="Adventure4.html">ADVENTURE IV. THE BOSCOMBE VALLEY MYSTERY</a>
</li>
<li id="Adventure5">
<a href="Adventure5.html">ADVENTURE V. THE FIVE ORANGE PIPS</a>
</li>
<li id="Adventure6">
<a href="Adventure6.html">ADVENTURE VI. THE MAN WITH THE TWISTED LIP</a>
</li>
<li id="Adventure7">
<a href="Adventure7.html">ADVENTURE VII. THE ADVENTURE OF THE BLUE CARBUNCLE</a>
</li>
<li id="Adventure8">
<a href="Adventure8.html">ADVENTURE VIII. THE ADVENTURE OF THE SPECKLED BAND</a>
</li>
<li id="Adventure9">
```

```
<a href="Adventure9.html">ADVENTURE IX. THE ADVENTURE OF THE ENGINEER'S THUMB</a>
</li>
<li id="Adventure10">
<a href="Adventure10.html">ADVENTURE X. THE ADVENTURE OF THE NOBLE BACHELOR</a>
</li>
<li id="Adventure11">
<a href="Adventure11.html">ADVENTURE XI. THE ADVENTURE OF THE BERYL CORONET</a>
</li>
<li id="Adventure12">
<a href="Adventure12.html">ADVENTURE XII. THE ADVENTURE OF THE COPPER BEECHES</a>
</li>
</ol>
</nav>
</body>
</html>
```

THE OPF FILE

We will now change the OPF file so that it is a EPUB 3 file.

Our current package element is:

```
<package xmlns="http://www.idpf.org/2007/opf" unique-identifier="SholmeskId" version="2.0">
```

The simplest way to change this to an EPUB 3 is to change the version number from "2.0" to "3.0". We can also add attributes as xml:lang and prefix to the <package> element. These attributes were not allowed in EPUB 2.

We need to add line to the metadata section which details when the last modification was made:

```
<meta property="dcterms:modified">2012-01-18T12:47:00Z</meta>
```

To make the changes for the new table of contents file we delete the references in the manifest for toc.ncx and toc.html and add a reference to toc.xhtml.

The toc.xhtml should have the attribute properties="nav" as in:

```
<item id="toc" properties="nav" href="toc.xhtml" media-type="application/xhtml+xml"/>
```

The <spine> element has got the attribute toc="ncx"

We remove this attribute.

We also change the reference in the <guide> element from toc.html to toc.xhtml.

The complete listing for our OPF is:

```
<?xml version="1.0" encoding="UTF-8"?>
<package xmlns="http://www.idpf.org/2007/opf" unique-identifier="SholmeskId" version="3.0">
<metadata xmlns:dc="http://purl.org/dc/elements/1.1/">
<dc:title id="title">The Adventures of Sherlock Holmes</dc:title>
<dc:creator id="creator">Sir Arthur Conan Doyle</dc:creator>
<dc:identifier id="SholmeskId">EPUBservicesco.com.sherlock-holmes</dc:identifier>
<dc:language>en</dc:language>
<meta property="dcterms:modified">2013-07-28T12:47:00Z</meta>
</metadata>
<manifest>
<item id="style" href="styles.CSS" media-type="text/CSS"/>
<item id="toc" properties="nav" href="toc.xhtml" media-type="application/xhtml+xml"/>
<item id="Adventure1" media-type="application/xhtml+xml" href="Adventure1.html"></item>
<item id="Adventure2" media-type="application/xhtml+xml" href="Adventure2.html"></item>
<item id="Adventure3" media-type="application/xhtml+xml" href="Adventure3.html"></item>
<item id="Adventure4" media-type="application/xhtml+xml" href="Adventure4.html"></item>
<item id="Adventure5" media-type="application/xhtml+xml" href="Adventure5.html"></item>
<item id="Adventure6" media-type="application/xhtml+xml" href="Adventure6.html"></item>
<item id="Adventure7" media-type="application/xhtml+xml" href="Adventure7.html"></item>
<item id="Adventure8" media-type="application/xhtml+xml" href="Adventure8.html"></item>
<item id="Adventure9" media-type="application/xhtml+xml" href="Adventure9.html"></item>
<item id="Adventure10" media-type="application/xhtml+xml" href="Adventure10.html"></item>
<item id="Adventure11" media-type="application/xhtml+xml" href="Adventure11.html"></item>
<item id="Adventure12" media-type="application/xhtml+xml" href="Adventure12.html"></item>
<item id="cover.xhtml" media-type="application/xhtml+xml" href="cover.xhtml"/>
<item id="SH_cover" href="images/cover.png" media-type="image/png"></item>
<item id="Ch_start_image" href="images/Holmes_with_glass.png" media-type="image/png"></item>
</manifest>
```

```
<spine>
<itemref idref="cover.xhtml"/>
<itemref idref="Adventure1"/>
<itemref idref="Adventure2"/>
<itemref idref="Adventure3"/>
<itemref idref="Adventure4"/>
<itemref idref="Adventure5"/>
<itemref idref="Adventure6"/>
<itemref idref="Adventure7"/>
<itemref idref="Adventure8"/>
<itemref idref="Adventure9"/>
<itemref idref="Adventure10"/>
<itemref idref="Adventure11"/>
<itemref idref="Adventure12"/>
</spine>
<guide>
<reference type="toc" title="Table of Contents" href="toc.xhtml"/>
</guide>
</package>
```

All other files in our project remain the same so we can now build and validate the eBook.

12 CALIBRE

Calibre describes itself as an eBook Library Manager. It can view eBooks, catalogue them, convert them from one format to another and talk to eReaders such as the Kindle. As someone who wants to create eBooks, the functionality you are interested is the ability to convert books. This allows you to take a book or document in one format such as HTML or a word processor format and convert this to the Kindle. However, you should be aware that Calibre has powerful functionality to manage your eBook collection.

INSTALLING CALIBRE

You can download Calibre from:

http://calibre-eBook.com/

When you run Calibre for the first time after it is installed you will be taken through the welcome wizard which helps you set the tool up on your machine.

The first step allows you select your language and decide where Calibre Library should be.

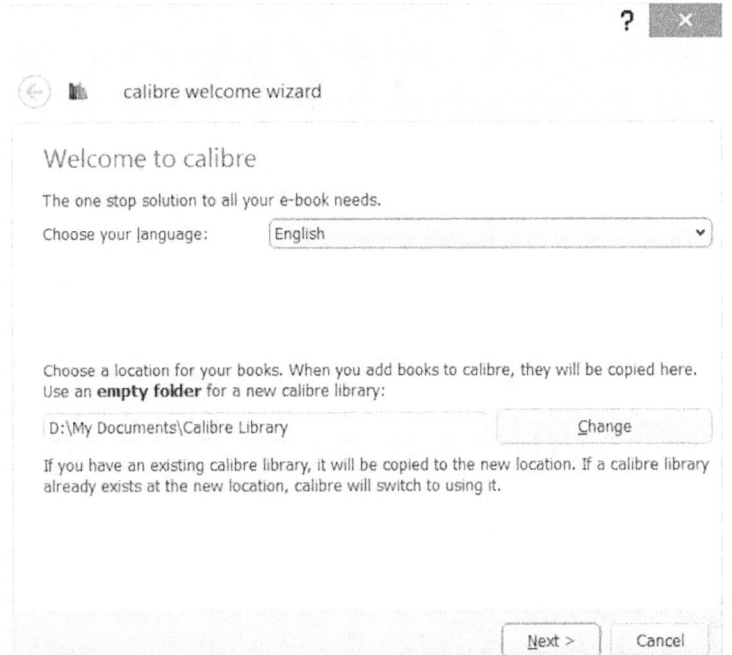

You can then choose the book device you usualy use.

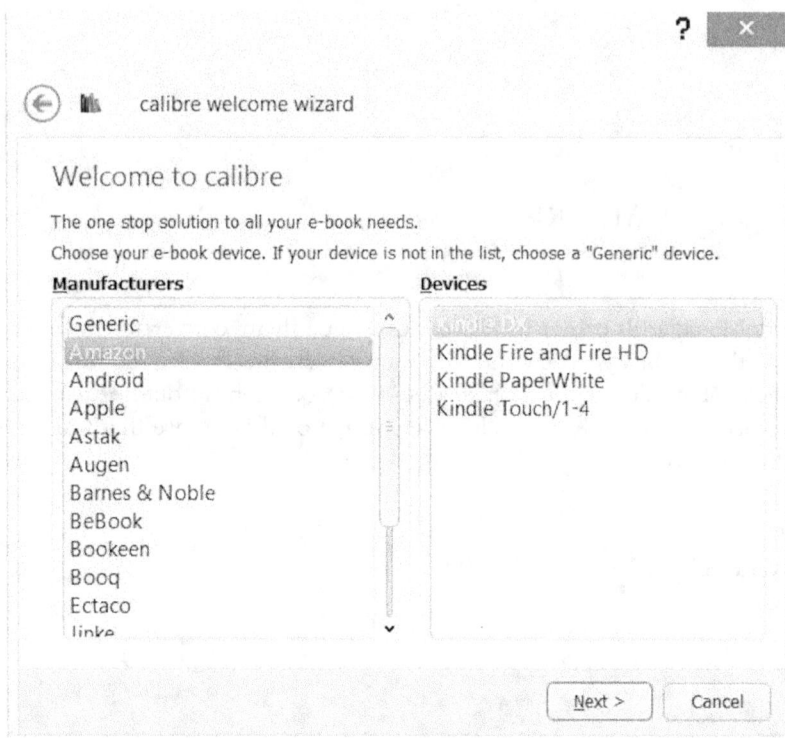

Calibre can automatically send email and this is where you would add the email account details.

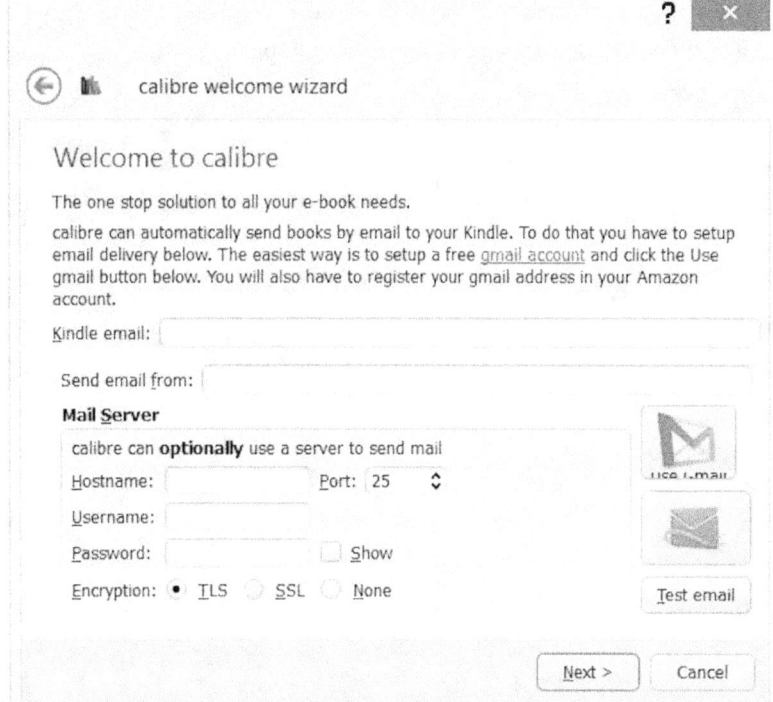

You have now completed installation and can watch an introductory video or just start working with Calibre.

? ☒

(←) calibre welcome wizard

Welcome to calibre

The one stop solution to all your e-book needs.

Congratulations!

You have successfully setup calibre. Press the Finish button to apply your settings.

Demo videos

Videos demonstrating the various features of calibre are available online.

User Manual

A User Manual is also available online.

Finish   Cancel

CALIBRE FUNCTIONALITY

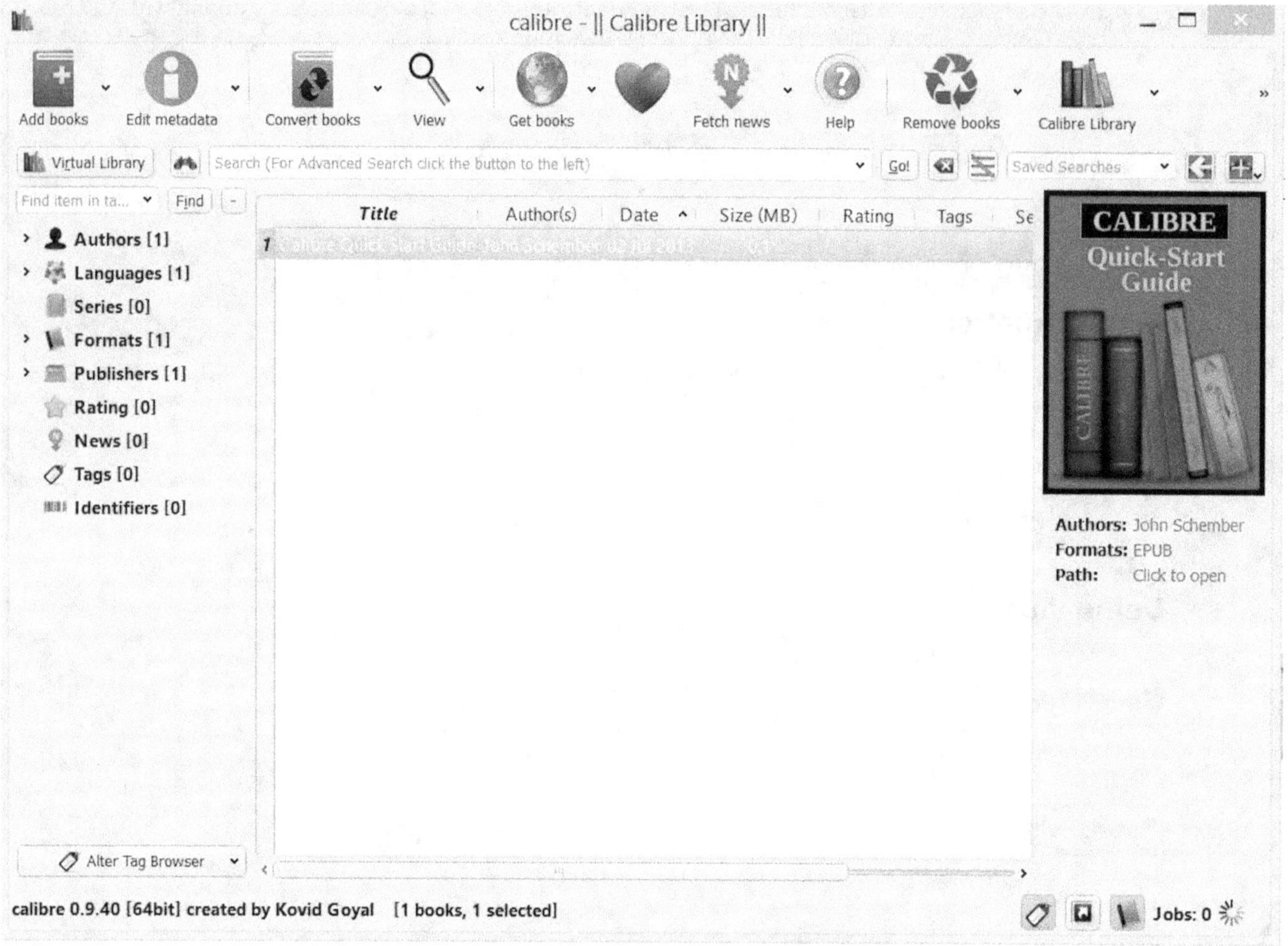

Add Books

This allows you to add books to Calibre. The "v" to the side of the icon allows you to select the sub-menu items listed in bold below. If you select the icon this will select the first sub-menu item "Add books from a single directory.

Add books from a single directory

This allows you a book in any of the different formats supported by Calibre. In the tutorial later we will be using this option to add a document in HTML format which we will convert to an eBook format. It is also possible to add documents in the Word or text formats.

Add book from directories, including subdirectories (One book per directory, assumes every eBook file is the same book in a different format)

This presumes that you are storing each eBook in a separate directory with an eBook directory. Calibre will add one book for each directory or subdirectory it finds. If there are several files in a particular subdirectory it will presume that the files are different formats for the same eBook.

Add book from directories, including subdirectories (Multiple books per directory, assumes every eBook file is a different book)

This presumes that you are storing each eBooks directories and subdirectories and each file represents a different eBook.

Add empty book (Book entry with no formats)

This allows you to create a new eBook which you can later add files, metadata and convert to an eBook. When you select this option you will see the dialog box below where you can tell calibre the following information:

- How many emplty books should be added?

- Set the author of the new books to:

- Set the series of the new books to:

-

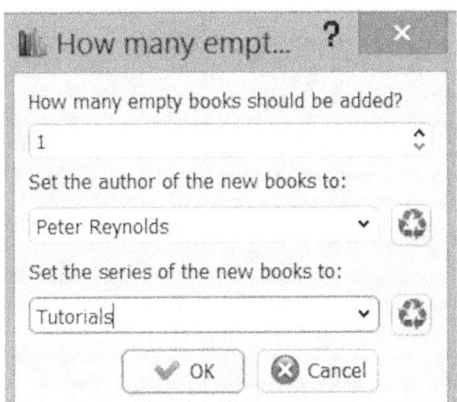

Add from ISBN

This allows you add one or more ISBN identifiers and Calibre will attempt to find and add the book

Add files to selected book records

This will allow you to add a file to the selected book.

Control the adding of books

This allow you to create rules for adding new books to your Calibre library.

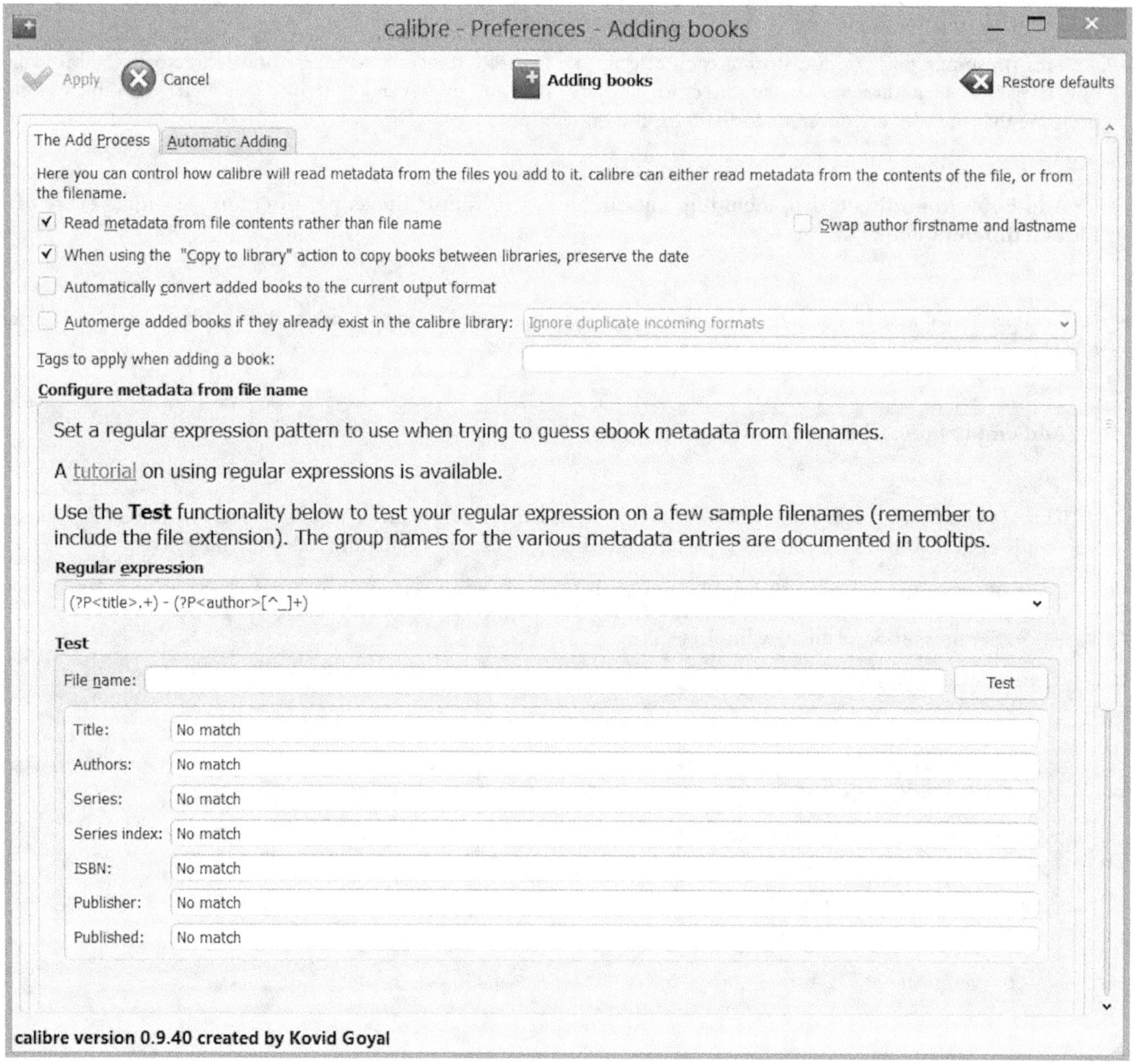

calibre - Preferences - Adding books

Apply   Cancel   **Adding books**   Restore defaults

The Add Process   Automatic Adding

Here you can control how calibre will read metadata from the files you add to it. calibre can either read metadata from the contents of the file, or from the filename.

☑ Read metadata from file contents rather than file name   ☐ Swap author firstname and lastname

☑ When using the "Copy to library" action to copy books between libraries, preserve the date

☐ Automatically convert added books to the current output format

☐ Automerge added books if they already exist in the calibre library: Ignore duplicate incoming formats   ⌄

Tags to apply when adding a book:

Configure metadata from file name

Set a regular expression pattern to use when trying to guess ebook metadata from filenames.

A tutorial on using regular expressions is available.

Use the **Test** functionality below to test your regular expression on a few sample filenames (remember to include the file extension). The group names for the various metadata entries are documented in tooltips.

Regular expression

(?P<title>.+) - (?P<author>[^_]+)   ⌄

Test

File name: Test

Title:	No match
Authors:	No match
Series:	No match
Series index:	No match
ISBN:	No match
Publisher:	No match
Published:	No match

calibre version 0.9.40 created by Kovid Goyal

Using this functionality you can make Calibre search for and eBooks automatically.

Edit metadata

Edit metadata

The Edit metadata function allows you to edit the metadata about the eBook. This includes edit information such as author, title, genre and adding and editing covers etc.

The submenu offer the following functionality:

Edit metadata individually

Selecting this option opens an editor for the metadata of the selected eBook. The Edit metadata icon on the toolbar will also open this dialog.

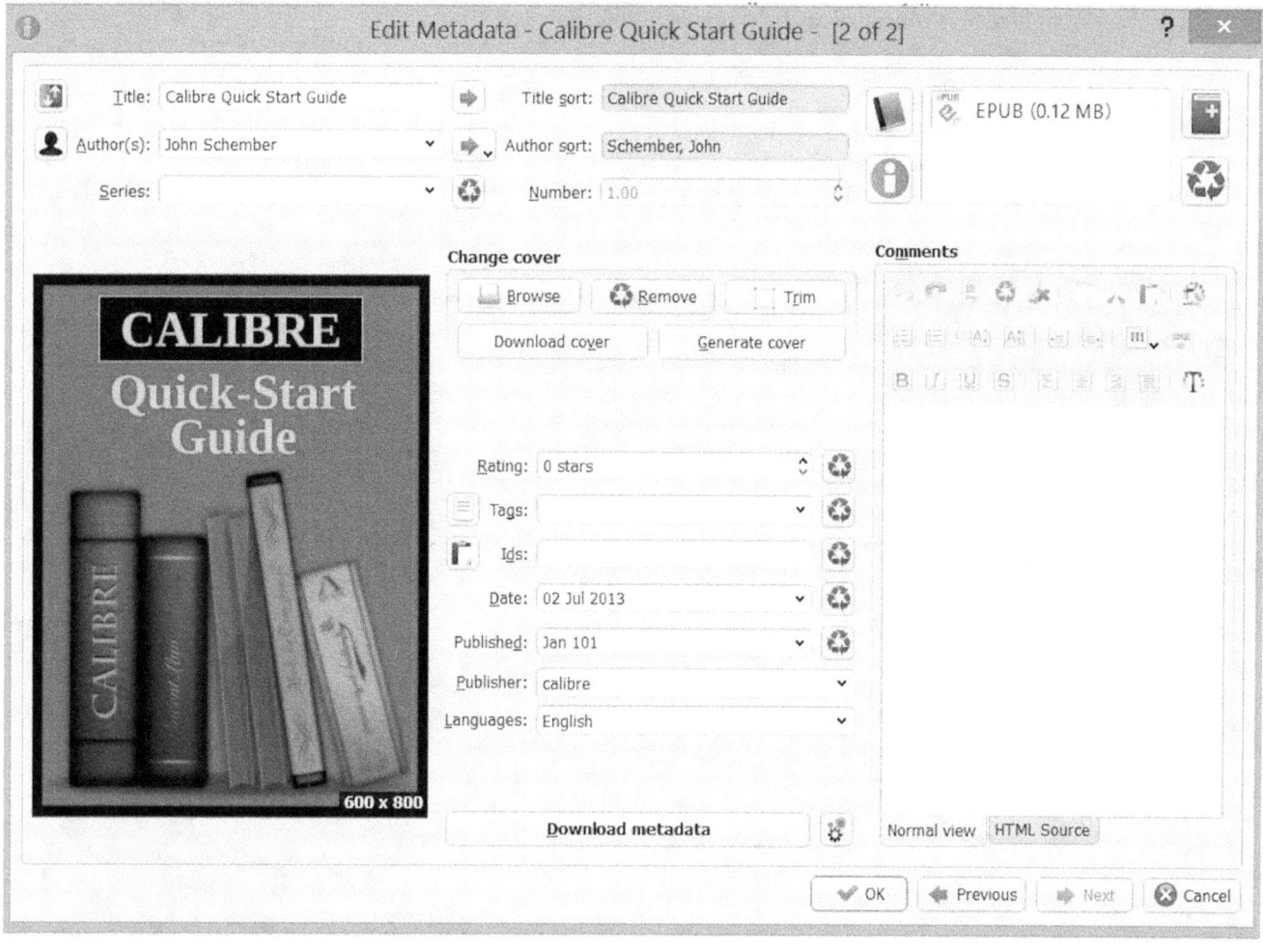

This dialog box allows you to enter and edit the metadata associated with a particular eBook including:

- Title

- Author

- Series

- Title Sort

- Author sort

- Number - version number

- Rating

- Tags

- ID - Such as ISBN identifier

- Date

- Date Published

- Publisher

- Languages

It is also possible to add covers to the book through this dialog box.

Edit metadata in bulk

The "Edit metadata in bulk" menu allows you to edit one or more eBooks you have selected in Calibre. There is also functionality here where you can select any number of books and do a search and replace on the metadata.

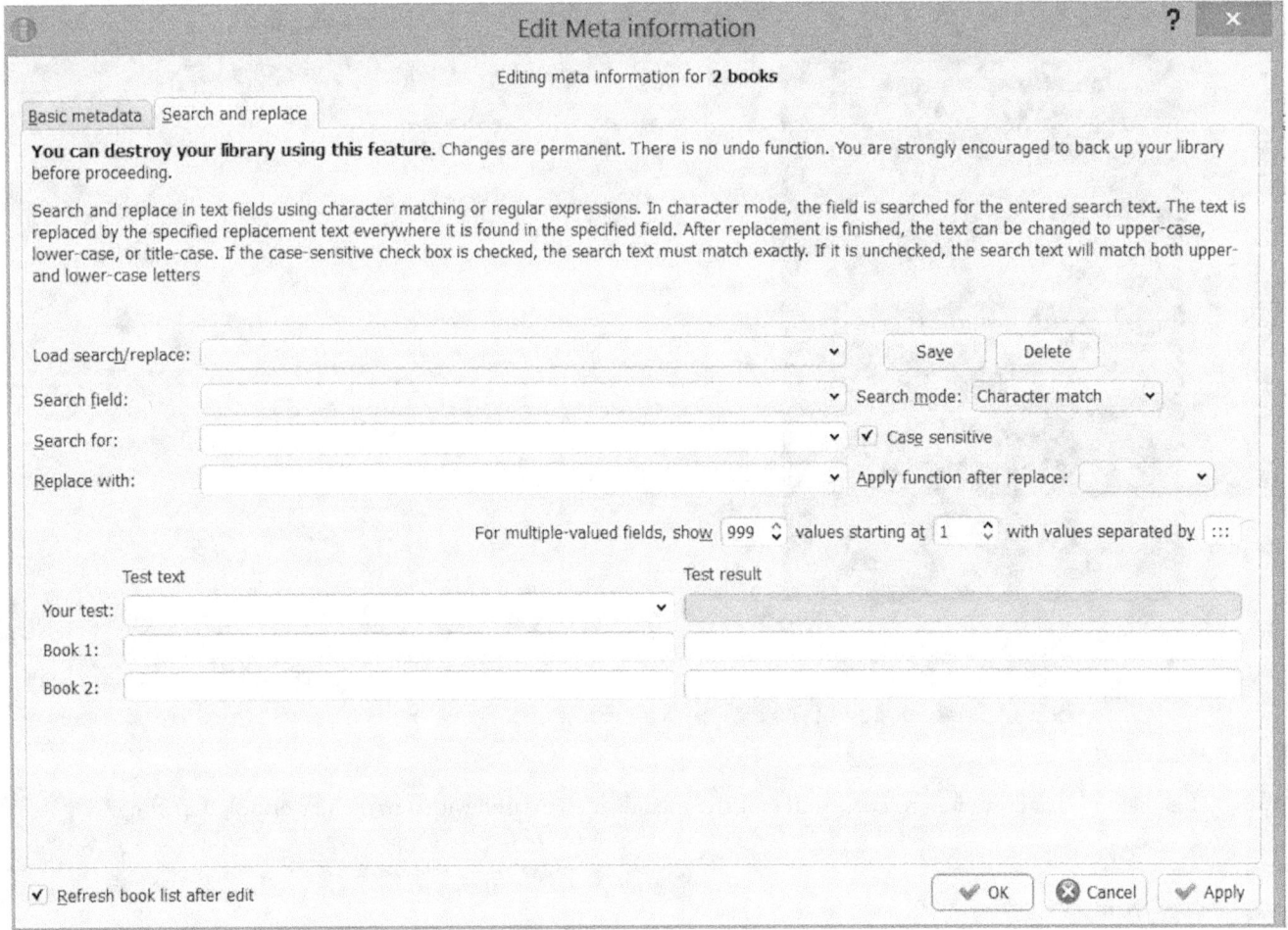

Download metadata and covers

This function allows you download the metadata and covers for the eBook or eBooks you have selected. You are given the option to download only the cover or only the metadata or both

Merge book records

This allows you to merge any number of eBooks into a single eBook. You are given the following options with this:

Merge into first selected book - delete others

Merge into first selected book - keep others

Merge only formats into first selected book - delete others

Convert books

Convert books

This functionality allows you the option of convert eBooks from one format to another. Calibre is able to convert books to and from the following formats:

Convert to

- EPUB
- mobi
- azw3
- fb2
- HTMLZ
- lit
- lrf
- pdb
- pdf
- pmlz

Convert from

- EPUB
- mobi
- azw3
- fb2
- HTMLZ
- lit
- lrf
- pdb
- pdf
- pmlz
- tpz
- azw1
- txt
- doc
- odt

- doc

- docx

- HTML

- snb

- cbz

- cbr

- cbc

- zip

- rar

The submenu offers the following functionality:

Convert individually

Bulk convert

Create a catalogue of the books in your Calibre Library

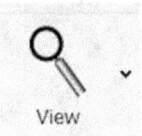

View

This item allows for you to view a book or newsfeed in the Calibre E-book Viewer.

The menus give you the opportunity to do the following:

View - view the currently selected book

View a specific format

Read a random book

Get books

The Get books function allows you to search for eBooks in particular eBook stores. The submenus give the following options:

- Search for eBook

- Search for this author

- Search for this title

- Search for this book

- Stores - This offer a choice of online eBook stores.

- Choose stores - This allows you to customize which store you to search in.

Donate

Calibre is free software but those involved in would appreciate your support if you love the tool. You can donate to Calibre at the following website: http://calibre-eBook.com/donate

Fetch news

Calibre has functionality which allows you to download RSS feeds from news website. The submenus allow for the following:

- Schedule News download

- Add a customer news source

- Download all scheduled news sources

Help

This provides you with a link to a website which contains the Calibre help.

Remove books

This allows you remove selected books from your Calibre library. The submenus allow to choose to remove all eBooks with a specific file format, remove all formats except one, remove covers and remove matching books.

Calibre Library

This allows you to select where you Calibre library is held. You can perform Library maintenance through the function.

Save to disk

This allows you to save your files to disk. You can also select which format to save.

Connect/ share

This allows you to manually connect to a device or folder on your computer. It also allows you to set up you calibre library for access via a web browser or email.

Preferences

This allows you to change the way Calibre works. Calibre has also a library of plugins which can be added through this dialog box.

13 TUTORIAL 5 BUILDING AN EBOOK WITH CALIBRE

We will again use Sir Arthur Conan Doyle's collection of short stories, The Adventures of Sherlock Holmes, for our tutorial. I have included the text for this book, which is out of copyright, with the tutorial files available at http://www.epubservicesco.com/book.html

The Tutorial will show you how to do the following:

- Convert a book from text to HTML in your word processor

- Formatting the Chapters

- Add illustrations

- Adding the book to Calibre

- Adding metadata

- Add a cover

- Add metadata

- Create a eBook

Convert a book from text to HTML in your word processor

We will use Microsoft Word to add some basic HTML code and create a separate HTML file for each chapter.

Microsoft Word allows you to do a global search and replace. It is also possible to search or replace paragraph marks by using the characters: ^p.

The first thing I will do is replace any cases where there are more than one paragraph mark with a single paragraph mark. Using Ctrl+H I call the search and replace dialog box and put '^p^p' in the search field and '^p' in the replace field. This will find all instances where there are two paragraphs and replace them with a single paragraph mark. There may be cases where there were more than paragraph marks in a row and because of this I will keep running this search and replace until there are no cases of double paragraph marks found.

I will then use the search and replace dialog box again and put '^p' in the search field and '</p>^p<p>' in the replace field. This will insert a closing paragraph element at the end of each paragraph and an opening one at the beginning. I select replace all. When this is complete a dialog will ask me whether I want to do the search and replace for the whole document. I select no. I will also add one further <p> at the beginning of the document.

I will create a single HTML file with all 12 stories. In my HTML editor I will create a file with the following content. I will highlight all the text in the word processor and copy this into the section where I have placed the text "COPY TEXT FROM WORD PROCESSER HERE".

```
<!DOCTYPE html>
<html xmlns="http://www.w3.org/1999/xhtml">
<head>
<title>The Adventures of Sherlock Holmes</title>
<link type="text/CSS" href="styles.CSS" rel="Stylesheet"/></head>
<body>


COPY TEXT FROM WORD PROCESSER HERE
</body>
</html>
```

I know want to highlight the beginning of each adventure. I will highlight this text using the HTML code <h1>. This stands for header one and it means that this text is the top level heading.

I have also adding a graphic with a silhouette of Holmes after each title and split the title so that the number of the story is in the first line and the actual title starts on the second.

The code for this is as follows:

```
<h1>ADVENTURE I. - A SCANDAL IN BOHEMIA</h1>
<p> </p>
<p><img src="Holmes_with_glass.png" alt="" /></p>
<h2>I.</h2>
```

The <h1> element which is used for the title is split by the line break element <br/>. The image is inserted using the HTML editor wizard for adding an image. This looks after the size etc. However, with the Kindle you could just leave out everything other than <img src="Holmes_with_glass.png">.

The <h2> element is used to highlight the subsections in some of these stories.

I will then save the HTML and open Calibre.

Adding HTML file to Calibre

After I have opened Calibre I select the Add book button and select my HTML file. This will then add this HTML file as a book. Calibre is able to get the title of the book through the title elements in the HTML file.

Adding metadata

When you open the metadata dialog box you will see that the only information there is the title. You should add "Sir Arthur Conan Doyle" as the author.

I have also created a picture file for the cover with the text "The Adventures of Sherlock Holmes", there is then a silhouette of Sherlock Holmes and the bottom of the picture has the text "Sir Arthur Conan Doyle". I will add this picture as the cover and after I have done this I will save the metadata by clicking OK.

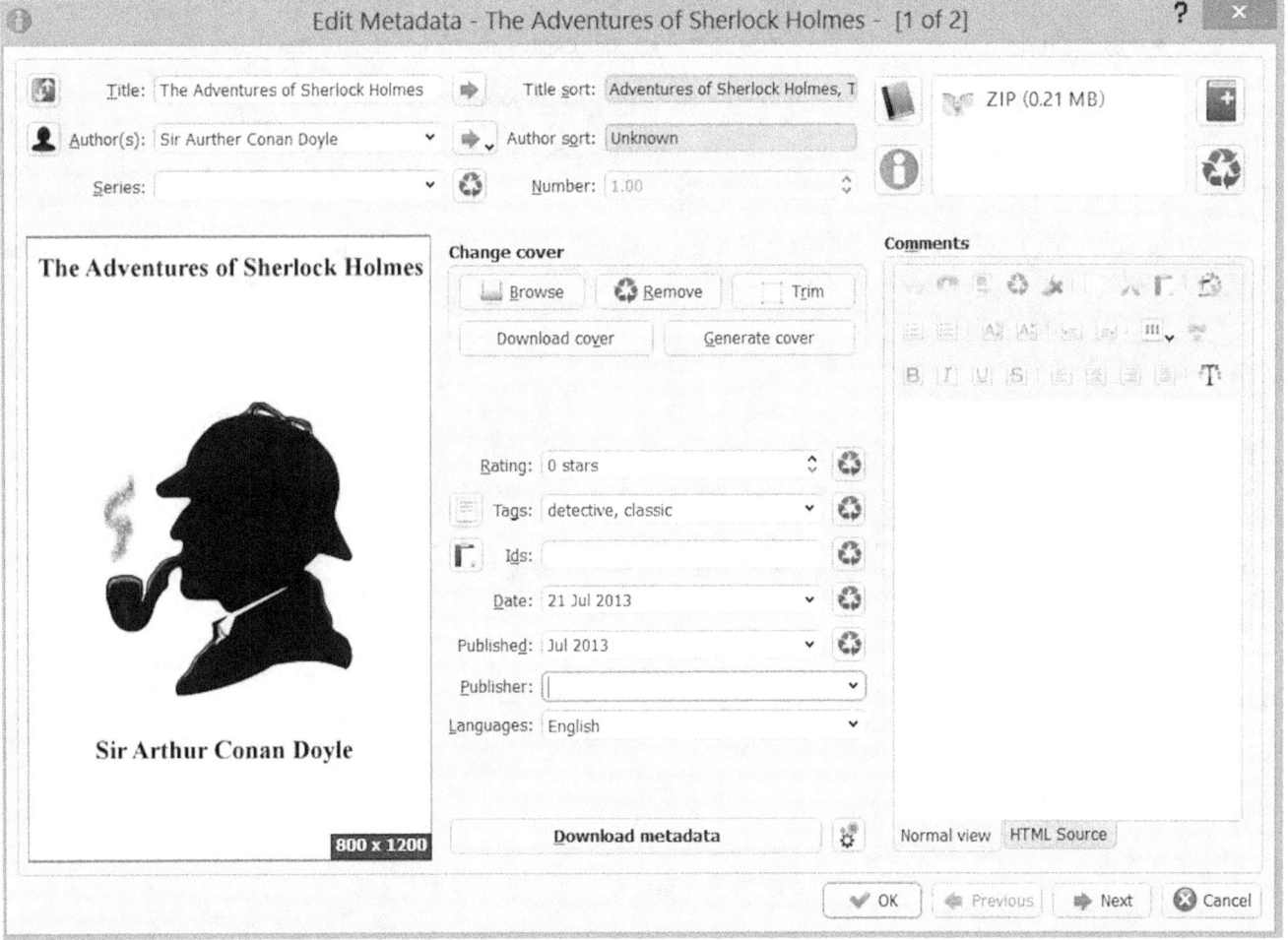

Converting the Book

When you are ready to build your book, highlight it in Calibre and select the Convert Book icon. You will see the dialog below. You should start by selecting your Output format which can be found in the top right corner of the dialog. In this case I have chosen Mobi.

The second last option shown on the left hand side is MOBI Output. If you changed the output format to some other option.

The Convert your book dialog has the following options:

- Metadata - This allows you to edit the metadata you have already entered.

- Look and Feel - This allows you to change the look and feel of the pages.

- Heuristic Processing - The allows you to detect and correct some common problems.

- Page Setup - This allows you to customize the output for your eReader.

- Structure Detection - Calibre will try to detect the structure of the book.

- Table of Contents - This allows for Calibre to automatically create a Table of Contents. I use the <h1> heading within my books for chapters. In this dialog box I select the wizard button to the right of the edit box which says level 1 TOC. In this dialog box I select <h1> from the drop down list called "Match HTML tags with tag name:". I also select the option to "Force use of auto-generated TOC"

- Search and Replace - This allows you to use regular expression for search and replace.

- MOBI Output - This allows you to choose some specific options for MOBI.

- Debug - This allows you to specify a folder where the debug files will be placed.

When you click OK Calibre will start building your book. You will see the Jobs icon in the bottom left hand corner working and when this is finished you can view the book by select the link above this

14 SIGIL

Sigil is a tool which set out to do one thing and that is create eBook in the EPUB format. Sigil has a built in editor so it possible to use the tool for writing your book as well as saving it im the EPUB format. If you are used to using word processors such as Microsoft Word it would probably be easier to use that and convert the file to HTML.

Preferences

The functionality which I would like to highlight is mainly located in tools menu. The one exception to this is the Preferences dialog located in the Edit menu.

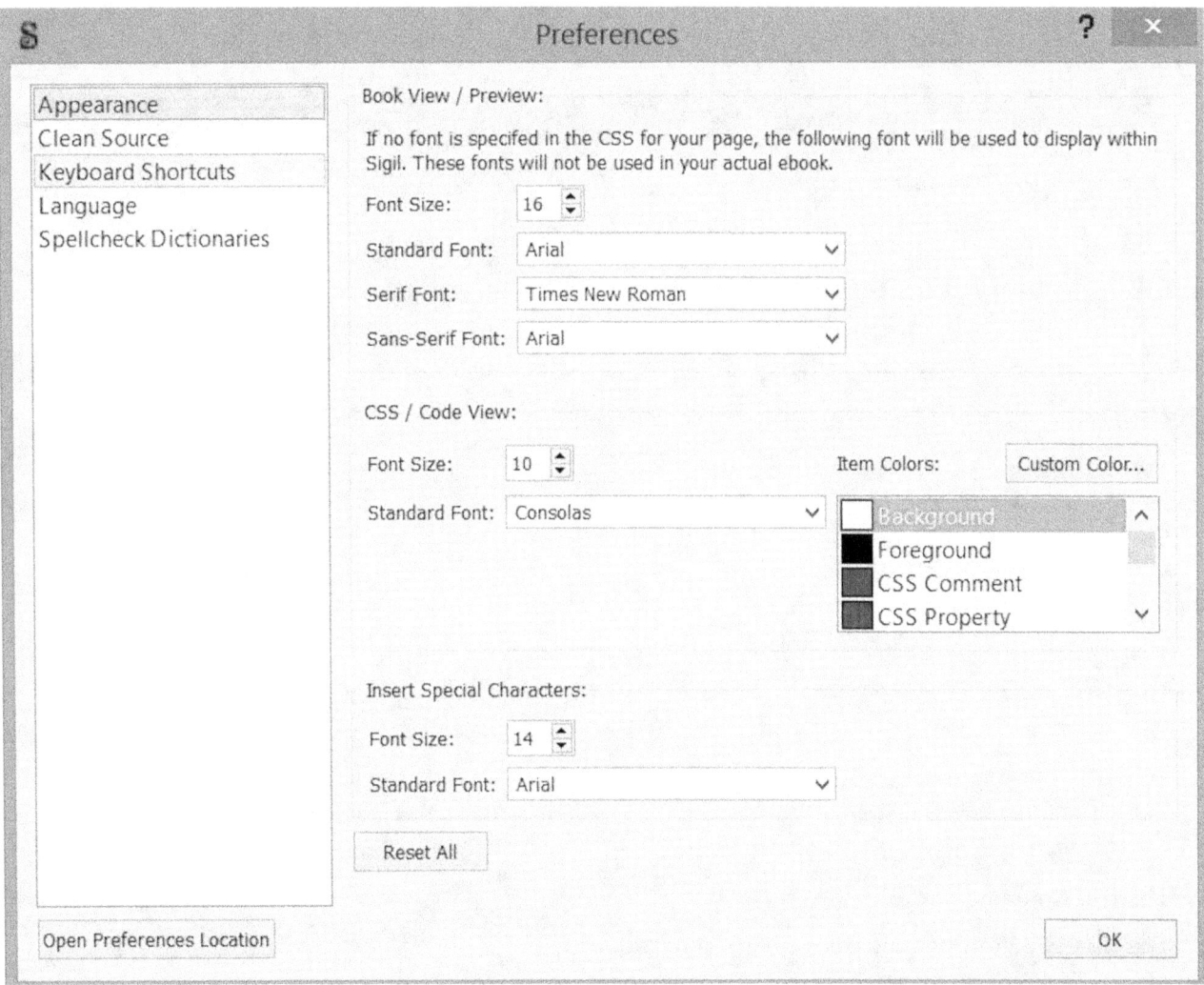

The Preferences dialog allows you to do the following:

- Appearance - This allows you to change the fonts which are used to display your book in Sigil. The tool does not use these fonts when creating an ebook.

- Clean Source - This allows you specify if your HTML code will be cleaned when it is opened and/ or saved. You can also choose whether you want Pretty Print Tidy or HTML Tidy to do the cleaning.

- Keyboard shortcuts - This allows you to modify the keyboard shortcuts used in Sigil.

- Language - You can change either the user interface language or the default language for metadata

- Spellcheck dictionaries - Sigil uses the Hunspell dictionaries which are widely used open source dictionaries. This dialog allows you to add your words to your dictionary and select from a number of dictionaries.

Add cover

This option which can be found at the top of the Tools menu does exactly what you would expect. You can specify an image file and Sigil will create a HTML cover page and use this in your ebook.

Metadata Editor

The Metadata Editor allow you to add and modify the metadata for your ebook. By selecting the Add Basic button you will be giving the option of adding metadata which is usually added to an ebook. By select the Add Role button you can add metadata for a specific type of contributor such author, editor or artist. The list of roles is comprehensive.

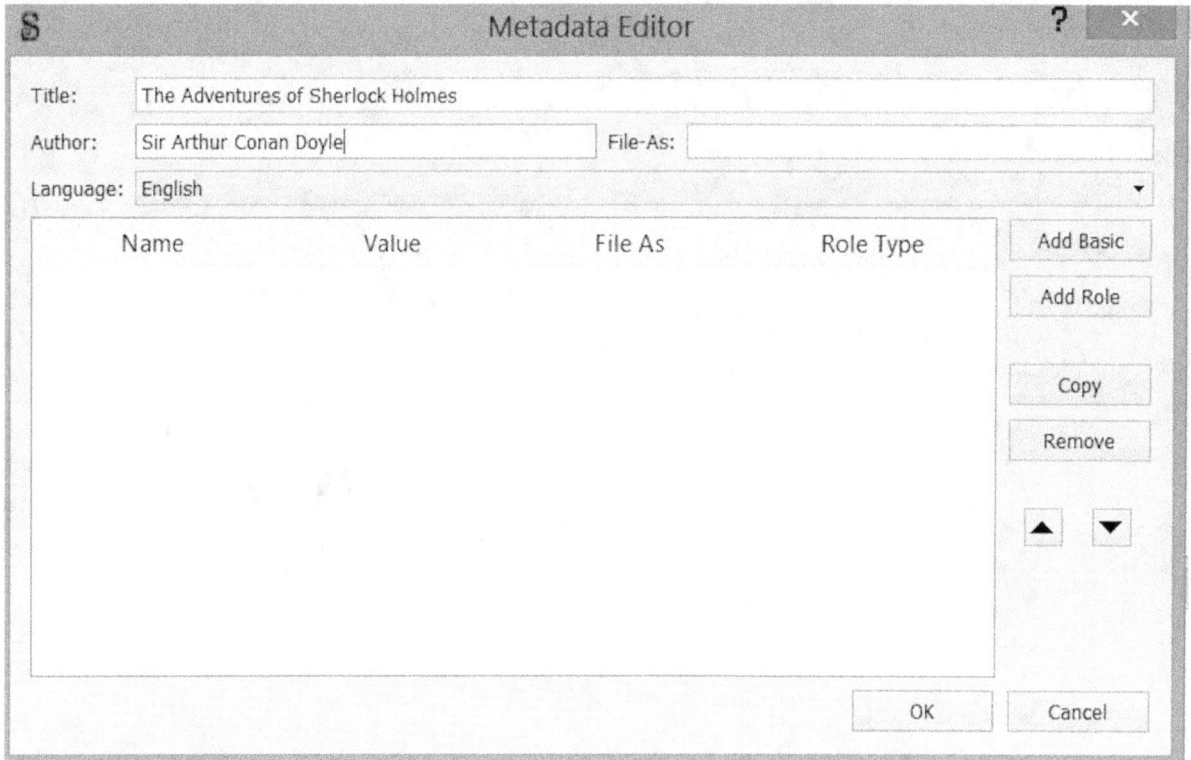

Table of Contents

This allows you to create and edit a table of contents.

Index

This allow you to create an index and add new terms to the index.

Spell check

This allows you to run the spell checker and control how it is used.

Validate EPUB with FlightCrew

This allows you to validate your EPUB book with FlightCrew. This is an open source EPUB validator http://code.google.com/p/flightcrew/ Please note that on the Sigil website they mention there maybe some things which FlightCrew do not detect and you can also use the IDPF EPUB validator http://validator.idpf.org/.

Validate stylesheets with W3C

This allows you to validate your CSS files against the W3C schema.

Reports

This gives you a report on the EPUB project.

Clip Editor.

Sigil allows you to add clip of code into your project. You can also add new clips, new groups and organize the clips.

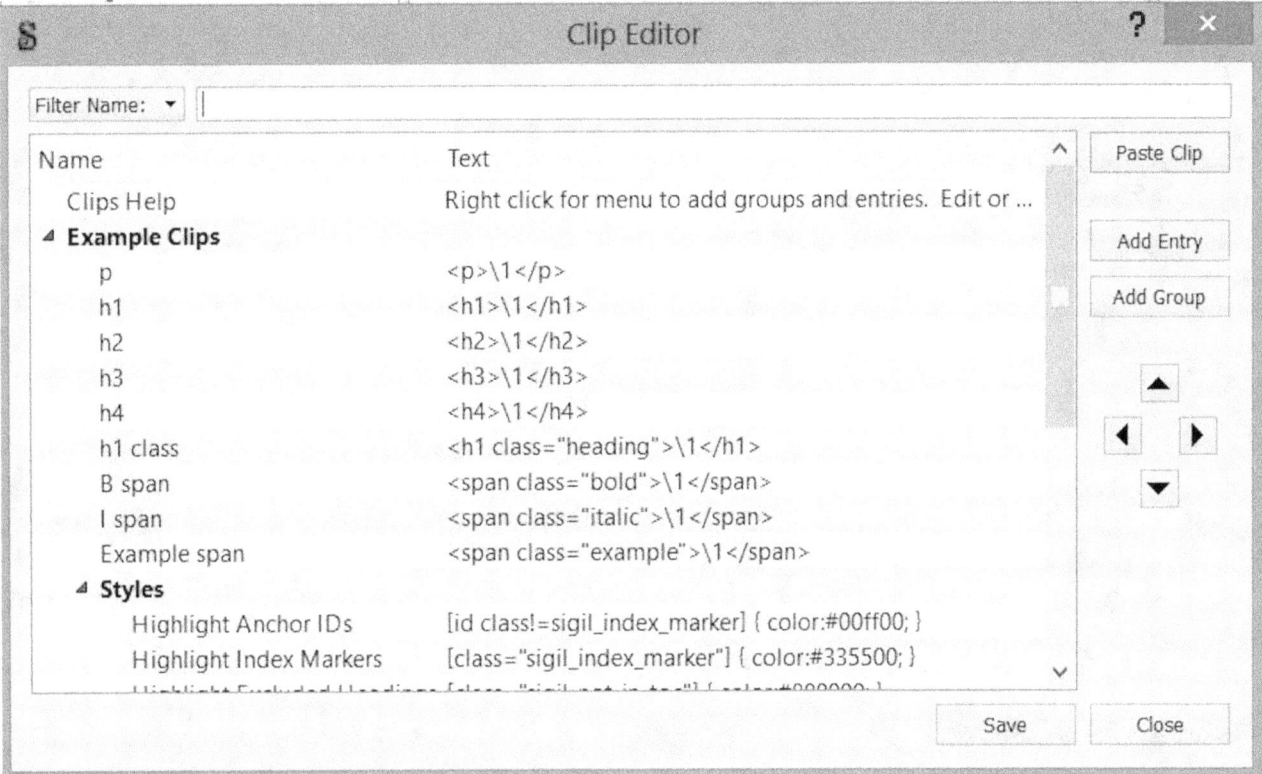

Saved Searches

This allows you to save and edit common find and replace searches. This is a particularly useful in looking for common mistakes made in HTML and other files.

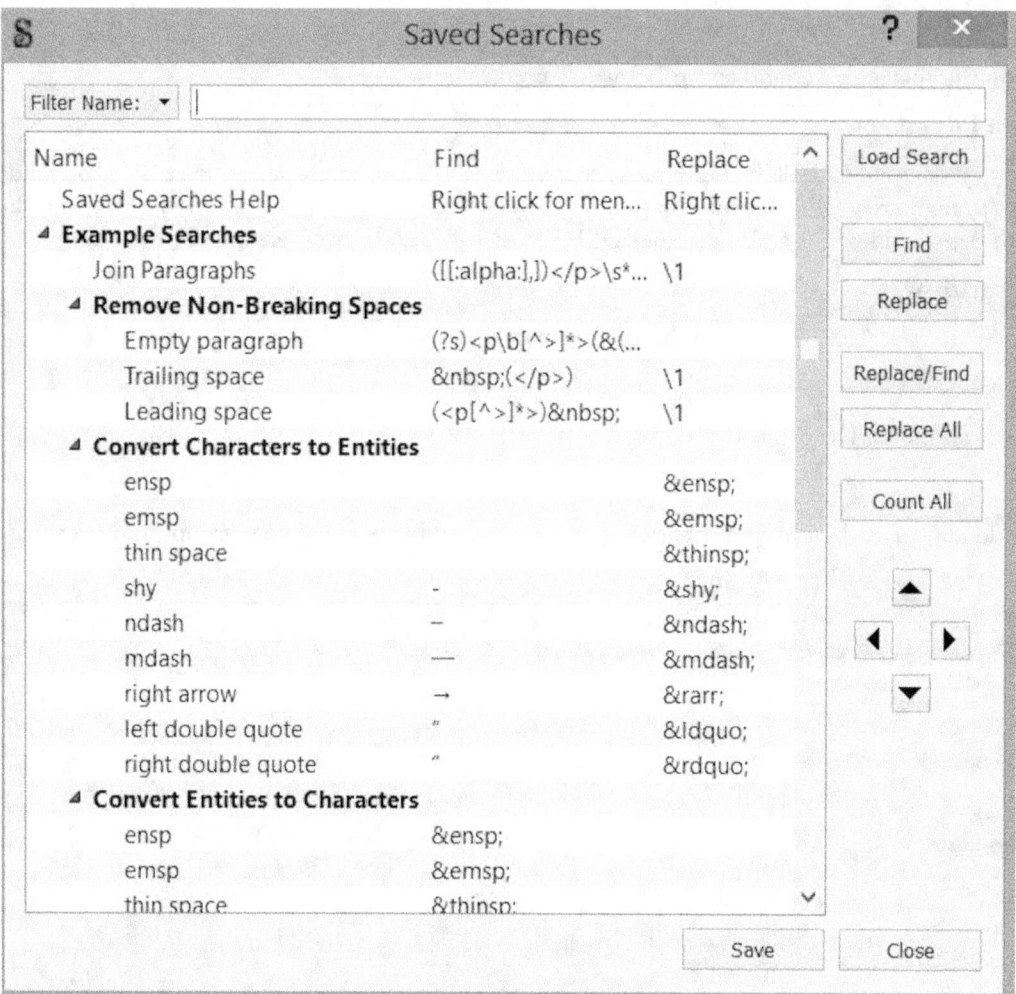

15 TUTORIAL 6 BUILDING AN EBOOK WITH SIGIL

In this tutorial we are going to use Sir Arthur Conan Doyle's book, "The Adventures of Sherlock Holmes". You can either create the HTML file using the method I have outlined in the first part of the Calibre tutorial or you can work with the document in Microsoft Word or another word processor and save the file as filtered HTML. In Word this is a way to create a "plainer" HTML than Word usually creates if saving the file as HTML. You should have highlighted the chapter heading as Heading 1 in Word before saving the file. If you wish to add a picture at the start of each chapter you should open this file in a HTML editor. Each Chapter heading will have been converted from the Heading 1 format used in Word to the <h1> element used in HTML. You can find the chapter headings by locating the <h1> element and after each of these add the following text:

<p><img src="Holmes_with_glass.png" alt="" /></p>

You should now open Sigil. When you do so you will a blank EPUB file.

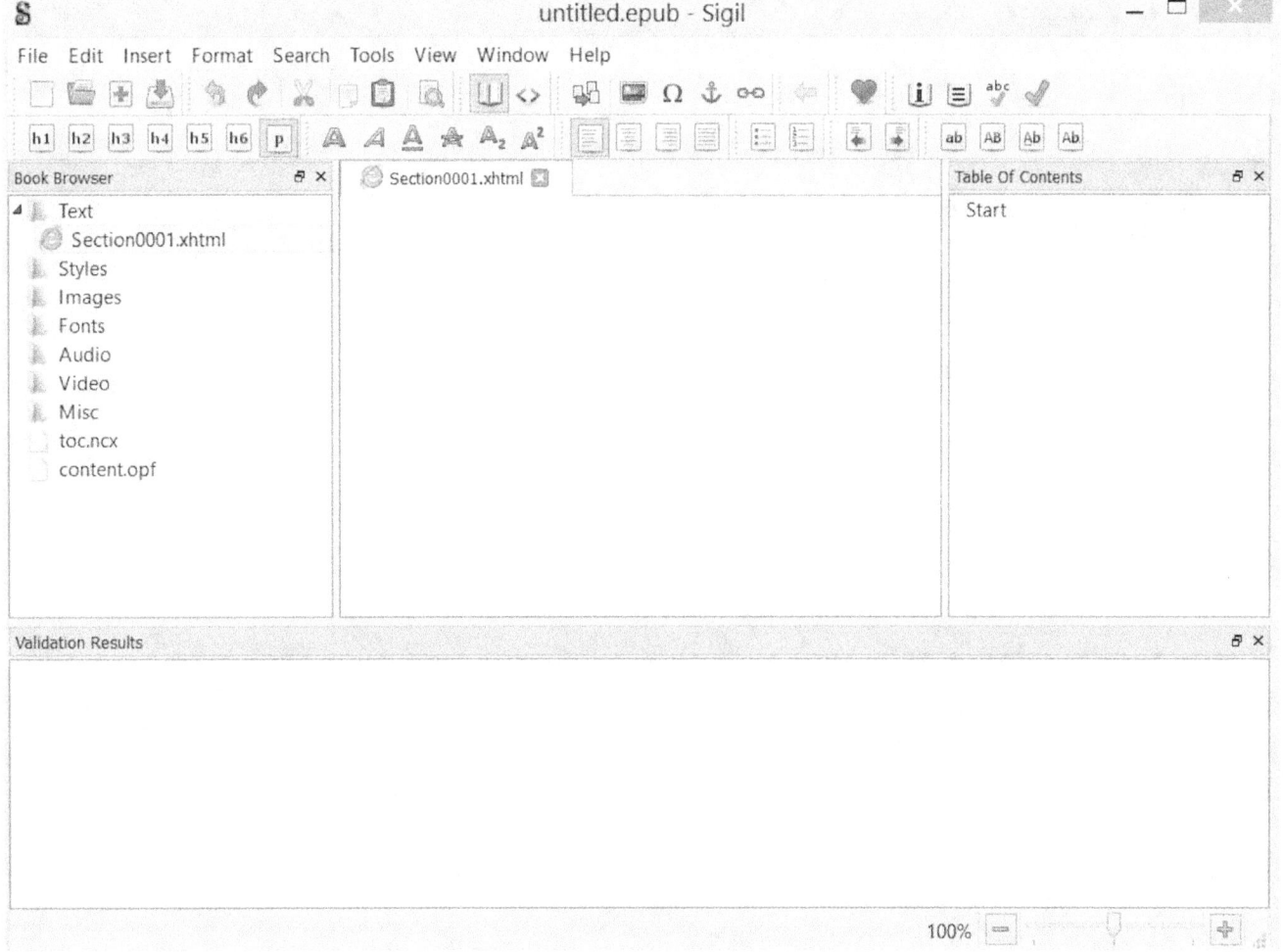

You should now add your HTML using File| Open which will then load the file in Sigil.

You should now create a Table of Contents by selecting Tool| Table of Contents | Generate Table of Contents. You will see everything which has been highlighted using , and so on.

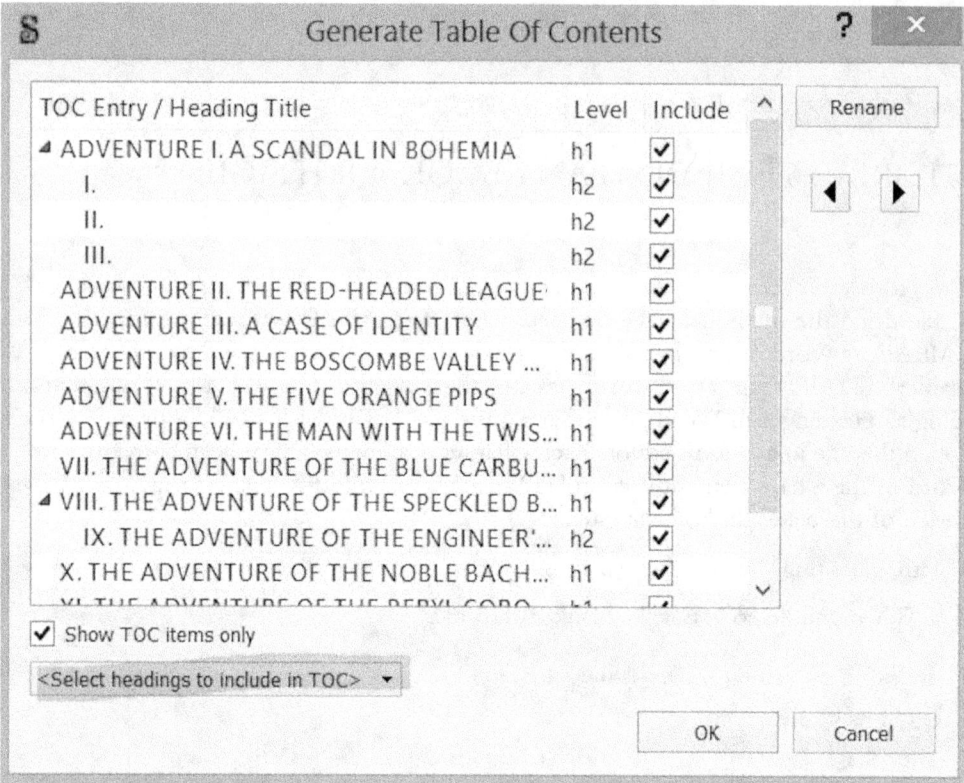

As we only want to use elements for the table of contents we select the button with the "" and in this menu choose "Up to level 1".

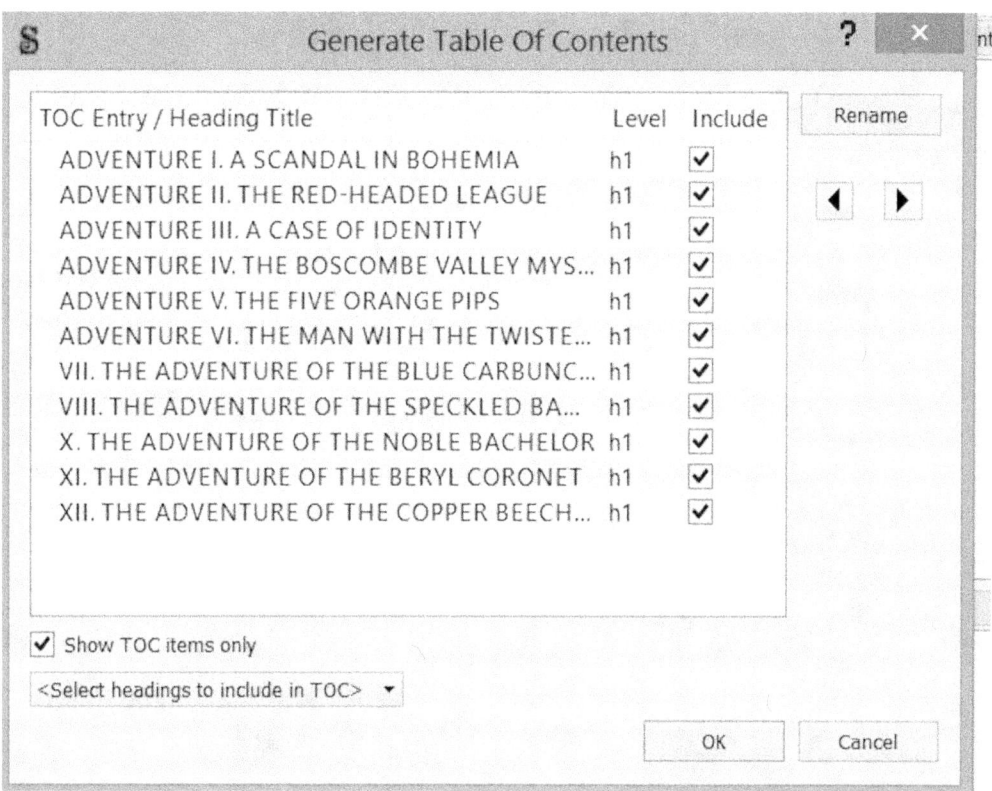

Then select OK.

The next step is to add metadata. We open the metadata editor by select Tools | Metadata Editor. We can then add metadata such as the title and author of the book as well as the name of the output file.

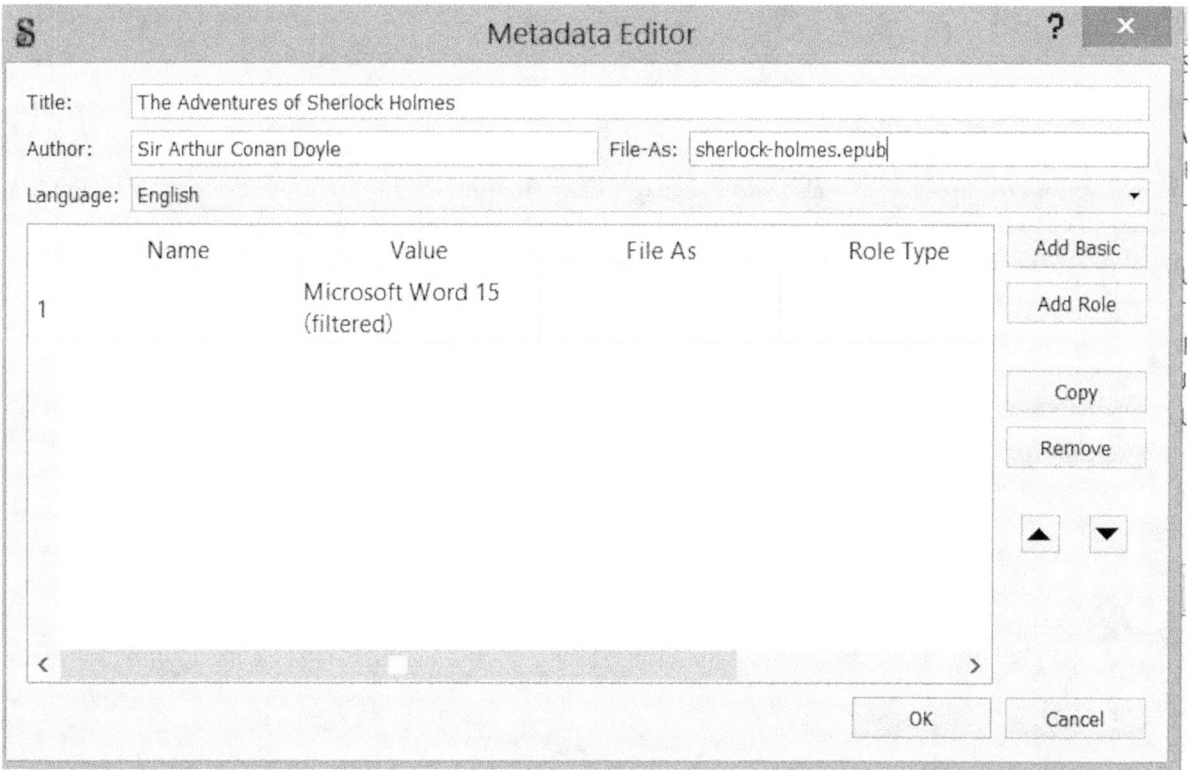

However, we will need to add further data and to do this we select the button "Add Basic".

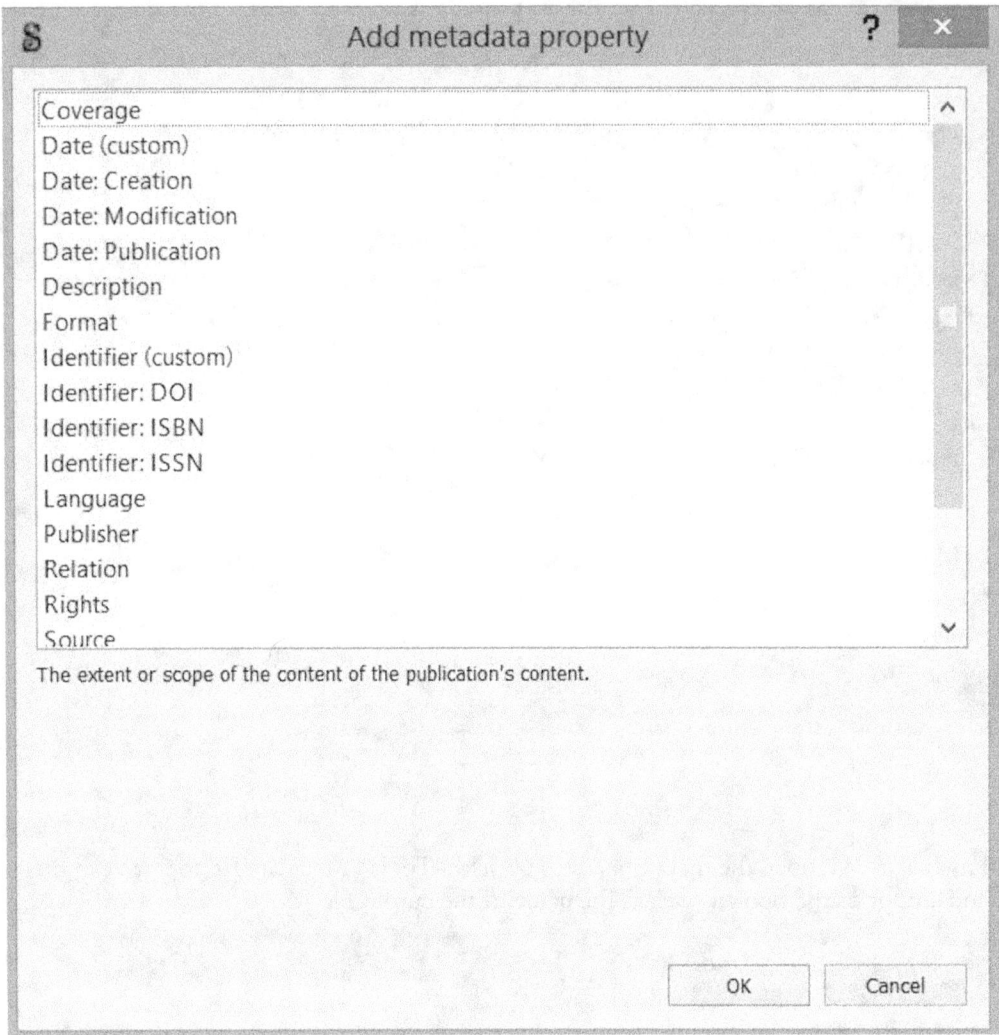

The EPUB format requires that you also add Language, Identifier (usually ISBN), Publisher and Date: Publication so we will add all of these.

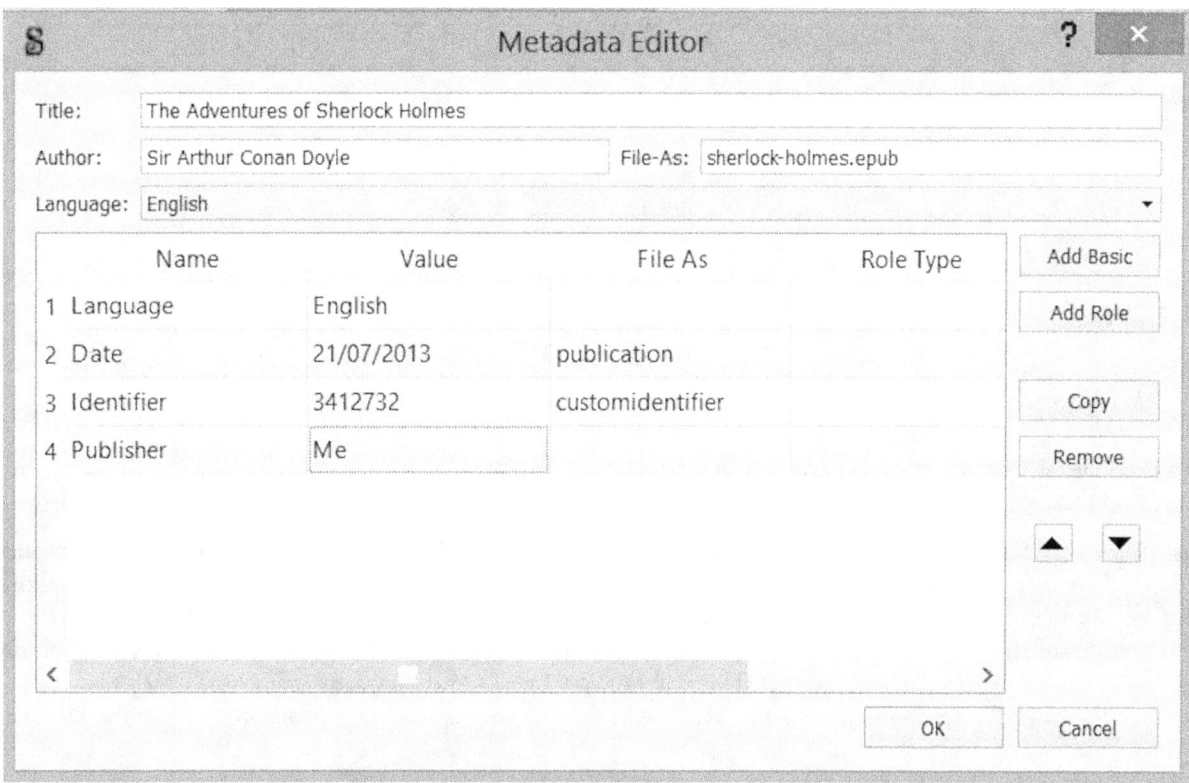

The book is now almost ready. Sigil offers a very useful validation function where you can check whether your book is a valid EPUB book. To do this Tools | Validate EPUB with FlightCrew. This takes the EPUB book sends it for validation and returns any errors which can then be fixed. If you get a "No Problems Found" message you can save your eBook by select File | Save as and saving the EPUB book.

16 PUBLISHING YOUR BOOK

When it comes to publish your book there will be certain information which will be needed by any of the services you use. I would recommend you thinking of these beforehand and having the information ready.

Tax - All the services listed below are US based services. If you have a US tax status you should have that number ready. If not then there is a relatively simple process for getting one. Amazon provide some useful information on this: Tax Information (If there is a problem with this link do a search for "tax information"on https://kdp.amazon.com). You will need a TIN (Taxpayer Identification Number). I would strongly recommend phoning the US tax office at +1 267 941-1099. This will save you weeks and they are usually able to tell you your TIN by the end of the call. If your country has a tax treaty with the US you can contact Amazon and pay the tax in your own country.

Book Information

Title

Is Book part of a series

Edition number

Publisher

Description - This is an opportunity to sell your book and you should put some effort into getting it right.

Book contributors - This is where you enter the names of authors and other contributors.

Language

Publication date

ISBN - If publishing with Amazon you do not need this if publishing with other providers you will. You will also need a separate ISBN for the printed and electronic version of your book.

Categories - This often presents difficulties for authors. They do not find their exact category in the list. I would recommend looking at the Amazon page for adding a new book and check out the categories there.

Keywords - Again this is crucial and you should think long and hard about. The only way that someone can buy your book is by finding out about and this is one of the paths to your future readers.

DRM - Digital Rights Management - This technology prevents a digital book being shared. However, most new authors want all the readership they can get and if someone shares a book with family and friends that increases the possibility of future sales.

Publishing rights - This confirms that you have the rights to publish the book and which regions you want to publish it in.

Royalty rate - Amazon have two rates 70% and 35%. The 70% is for books priced between $2.99 and $9.99 and the reason why you might want to opt for the 35% instead is that you want to sell your book for less. Amazon also charge for downloading files when the royalty rate is 70% but this is a good problem to have as more downloads means more sales. Details of Amazon's pricing policy is available here: Amazon Pricing Information

Kindle select - If you choose to include your book in Kindle Select it means you offer five days free promotion every three months. This is an excellent marketing opportunity. Kindle select also allows your books to be loaned though Kindle Prime and this is a very strong source of revenues. The negative side of this is that you have to agree to have your book sold exclusively on Amazon for at least three months and you need to exit the program before selling your books elsewhere. Amazon will remove your book from sale within five days. It is a good idea not to select the auto renewal button as this way your books can come out of Kindle Select after the 90 days and if you are happy with it you can renew them.

Amazon Kindle Direct

Amazon's self-publishing portal is called Kindle Direct Publishing and you can access it here: https://kdp.amazon.com/ I would recommend that you look at the information provided by Amazon. The have several free Kindle books on publishing on Amazon and building books for the Kindle as well as a help section: https://kdp.amazon.com/self-publishing/help/

Amazon are such a huge force in selling digital books that you cannot ignore them. The issue which I believe you have to consider is whether or not to Join Kindle Select. There are lots of different views and good reasons for and against doing it. You have to make the jusdgement.

Smash Words

Smash Words, http://www.smashwords.com/, is another web portal which will allow you to publish your material without difficult. The CEO and founder of Smash Words, Mark Cooper, has written an excellent style guide which you should read if you want to publish on Smash Words, or anywhere else for that matter: http://www.smashwords.com/books/view/52

Smash Words recommends that you upload a Microsoft Word file which has been formatted according to the instructions in their style guide. They will then covert it to eBook formats. Interestingly, the Kindle mobi format is one of the most popular formats there. You may also upload an ePub but this is beta version.

Smash Words publishes books on their own website and distributes them to the following resellers: Apple, Barnes & Noble, Diesel eBook Store, Kobo, Sony Reader Store, Baker & Taylor's Blio.com and the Aldiko e-reading app on Android.

It is possible to charge nothing for you book on Smash Words which is not possible with KDP.

Barnes & Noble Nook Press

Barnes and Noble's Nook Press website, https://www.nookpress.com/ , is their service for independent publishers and authors. An interesting feature of Nook Press is you can write your book on the online word processor which is part of the website. Like the other websites Nook Press has a good support section https://www.nookpress.com/support

RESOURCES

The Tutorial files used in the book are available from the following website: http://www.EPUBservicesco.com/book.html Please note that you should use the files in Tutorial 1 for the Calibre and Sigil Tutorials.

Kindle

Kindle Direct Publishing https://kdp.amazon.com/

Kindle Format http://www.amazon.com/kindleformat

Kindlegen http://www.amazon.com/kindleformat/kindlegen

Other tools

Mobipocket: http://www.mobipocket.com/dev/default.asp This company created the mobi format and then sold this to Amazon.

Calibre website: http://calibre-eBook.com/

Sigil website: http://code.google.com/p/sigil/

Sigil developers blog: http://sigildev.blogspot.com/

EPUB

IDPF (International Digital Publishing Forum): http://idpf.org/

EPUB 3 http://idpf.org/EPUB/30

EPUB 2.0.1 http://idpf.org/EPUB/201

EPUB 3 samples: http://code.google.com/p/EPUB-samples/

Transforming NCX into EPUB 3 Navigation Documents: http://blog.threepress.org/2011/06/14/ncx-into-EPUB3/

Book sellers

KDP https://kdp.amazon.com

Smash Words: http://www.smashwords.com/

Nook Press: http://www.nookpress.com/

Sony's eReader publisher's portal: https://eBookstore.sony.com/publishers/

ABOUT THE AUTHOR

Peter Reynolds is an Irish writer. He lives with his family, two corgi dogs and a ginger cat. Little Bad Wolf is his first book. Peter's day job is working in the translation and localisation industry where he is director of translation technology company. He is also very involved in developing industry standards at ISO and OASIS. Peter's book, Light A Big Fire, is a complete guide to building eBooks for the kindle.

www.ingramcontent.com/pod-product-compliance
Lightning Source LLC
Chambersburg PA
CBHW081507170526
45166CB00008B/2582